The Contemporary Condition book series offers a sustained inquiry into contemporaneity as a defining condition of our historical present. Departing from the assumption that the relationship between artistic practice and sociopolitical reality is undergoing substantial changes, the series centrally explores the coming into being of planetarity, the aesthetics and sensing of eco-systemic changes, and how the networked image can be understood as a relational assemblage to address the politics of infrastructure and wider ecologies.

I0418944

Sternberg Press

THE CONTEMPORARY CONDITION

THE CONTEMPORARY CONDITION 19

Challenging Institutionalization
A propositional toolkit for doing supervision of artistic
and practice-based research by Barbara Bolt, Maibritt Borgen,
Geoff Cox, Laura Guy, Maria Hlavajova, Maureen de Jager,
LEE Wing Ki, Christa-Maria Lerm Hayes, Glenn Loughran,
Jacob Lund, Mari Mäkiranta, Andrea Phillips, Henk Slager,
Alexandra R. Toland, Iris van der Tuin, and Mick Wilson

Edited by Maibritt Borgen, Iris van der Tuin, Jacob Lund,
and Henk Slager

Published by Sternberg Press, 2024

Series edited by Geoff Cox and Jacob Lund

Published in partnership with the Centre for Research in Artistic
Practice under Contemporary Conditions at Aarhus University,
made possible by the Novo Nordisk Foundation investigator grant
NNF21◊C0068539, 2022–2026. The publication of this volume is
funded by the Novo Nordisk Foundation Visiting Professorship in
Art & Art History Grant for Iris van der Tuin NNF21◊C0068560.

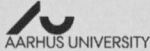

AARHUS UNIVERSITY

novo nordisk
foundation

Design: Dexter Sinister
Proofreader: Raphael Wolf
Printing and binding: Tallinn Book Printers, Estonia
Paper: Caribic 354-39 / Olin Light Blue

ISBN 978-1-915609-62-5

Sternberg Press
71–75 Shelton Street
London WC2H 9JQ
www.sternberg-press.com

Distributed by The MIT Press, Art Data, Idea Books,
and Les presses du réel

Challenging Institutionalization

A propositional toolkit for doing supervision of artistic and practice-based research by Barbara Bolt, Maibritt Borgen, Geoff Cox, Laura Guy, Maria Hlavajova, Maureen de Jager, LEE Wing Ki, Christa-Maria Lerm Hayes, Glenn Loughran, Jacob Lund, Mari Mäkiranta, Andrea Phillips, Henk Slager, Alexandra R. Toland, Iris van der Tuin, and Mick Wilson

Contents

PREFACE: PRACTICES *AS* PROPOSITIONS
Maria Hlavajova

Considered from the perspective of the theory-informed,
politically driven art institution that is BAK, basis voor actuele
kunst in Utrecht, the research imperative in contemporary
art concerns not merely some ontological reflection upon
the world nor a critical assessment of it that reproduces its
status quo; it is rather a matter of radical commitment to
this very world. A commitment that engages — concomi-
tantly — thinking how things are, imagining them otherwise,
and enacting these imaginaries as if they were possible.
I have often dubbed BAK's mission with these very words,
especially when pondering the role of art in the face of the
morbid symptoms that define the present — ecological disaster
and multiple wars the world over included — reasserting time
and again systemic inequalities and injustices into the lives
of people and the planet. How do we create, labor, and live
in such circumstances, and exist not merely against but
in spite of them?

Emerging alongside the ideals of social and ecological
justice, this practice of "thinking how things are, imagining
them otherwise, and enacting these imagines as if they
were possible" in spite of the way of the world has been the
political project of "instituting otherwise" at BAK. It fore-
grounds practices that do not depict or represent but rather
conspire where art, knowledge production, and social action
intersect. A collective practice of coming together in, with,
and through art, I see it as *practicing propositions* of what
does not yet exist: a just society in which a livable life-in-
common is possible.

While I write from the space of experimentation with
research and pedagogical agendas that engage the conditions
of the world from outside of academia, how does one attempt

to teach and supervise such artistic and practice-based research in the context of the university?

This very core question has shaped the summer school "Supervising Artistic and Practice-Based Research," which we at BAK were honored to host in the summer of 2023, together with a consortium consisting of Centre for Research in Artistic Practice under Contemporary Conditions, Aarhus University; The Laboratory for Art Research, The Schools of Visual Arts, The Royal Danish Academy of Fine Arts, Copenhagen; and Utrecht University. It convened with PhD and postdoc supervisors from across Europe and beyond to reflect on and challenge the existing formal educational pathways for artistic and practice-based research. The gathering aimed to develop collective and collaborative mappings of *practices* and *propositions* into a toolkit for researchers, supervisors, and evaluators to experiment with concrete pathways for pedagogical approaches—and commitments of artistic and practice-based research—to societal and planetary urgencies of our era.

This publication offers a vista onto the practices and propositions that shaped the exchanges during what has, in my view, become an extraordinarily inspiring gathering during the summer school. Seeking ways to navigate across the interstices of possibility in—and in spite of—the neoliberal educational-industrial complex of late, they cast forward the realities of urgent social, economic, and ecological challenges into pedagogical formats. In doing so, the faux distinction between practices and propositions, along which we as organizers structured the school's curriculum, gradually ceases to exist. One encounters instead the radical politics of generative learning, as well as a prefigurative research space that involves collectively practicing a comprehensive and nuanced imagination about what ultimately makes for a good university, and with it perhaps even a good society.

This is achieved by thinking how things are, imagining them otherwise, and embodying that imagination as if it were —and until it is—possible.

NOT ONE TOOLKIT, BUT MANY
Maibritt Borgen, Iris van der Tuin, Jacob Lund, and Henk Slager

You are holding in your hands a publication that is a toolkit.
Or perhaps, one could argue, a series of propositions for
toolkits (and propositions-as-toolkits) where each individual
contribution performs an actual toolkit, and the book itself
articulates a different kind of practice. That's our editorial hint
for how to make your way through this volume modularly.
Dig into it bit by bit, make its individual elements work for you
in your current situation. Poach, perhaps, as you read, in the
spirit of Michel de Certeau, who described readers as "travellers; they move across lands belonging to someone else, like
nomads poaching their way across fields they did not write."[1]

Who is invited, then, to poach here? This book is
written for and by supervisors of practice-based arts research
PhD and postdoc projects, and for those whose work rests
in and embraces the fruitful yet often unusual place of the
interface between art and academia: an environment where
artistic practice can be articulated and developed forcefully
as research, and where what Barbara Bolt describes as
the "work of art" becomes an important contribution to knowledge. But it is also the place where artistic and cultural practices intersect with neoliberal logistical management systems,
haunted by the ghost of what Laura Guy emphasizes as
the "measure of value" seeps in, "couched in the language
of innovation." In this institutional ecosystem artistic practice
meets practices of validation and oftentimes translation
into writing, all aspects that provide art with an additional
dimension and temporality. From here, one might poach the
experiences, advice, and practices of others.

1. Michel de Certeau, *The Practice of Everyday Life* (Berkeley: University of
California Press, 1984), 174.

In that way, one could read *Challenging Institutionaliza-tion* as both an invitation to and articulation of community. You will find threads of participation, kinship, and comradery running through the texts. Because the truth is that the place between art and academia can be lonely, and just as art is not created in a vacuum, neither are good supervisory practices. Most often, you are one or a few people at an institution.

This publication came out of a 2023 summer school in Utrecht, the Netherlands that sought precisely to bring people together and foster community. It can be seen as a collective mapping of this summer school into a constructive toolkit that brings together a plurality of voices. You can read the contributions diffractively, focusing on how they broaden or deepen each other, or use them individually to shape solidarity.

Challenging Institutionalization also contains an actual toolkit that can be used for situations of supervision or assessment, by supervisors and PhD researchers alike. This toolkit for artistic and practice-based researchers, supervisors, and evaluators provides a multilayered approach to formulating and reflecting on the conditions of the research both during the process itself and afterwards. Researchers, in conversation with their peers and/or supervisors, are invited to set the conditions of the research by working with two groups of interlinked questions. The toolkit supports a prospective and retrospective reflective process that respects the performative — nonlinear and unpredictable — process of artistic research. A first draft of this toolkit titled "Setting and reflecting on the conditions from within: A prospective and retrospective toolkit for artistic and practice-based researchers and their supervisors" was developed in between Denmark and the Netherlands in 2021 and 2022 by Jacob Lund, Iris van der Tuin, and Maibritt Borgen. The toolkit took inspiration from and was developed in dialogue with Barbara Bolt and Henk Slager. We invite you to bring this toolkit along in your practice as a supervisor to develop and enrich each individual project through dialogue.

Toolkitting as a verb is a sign of our algorithmic times. While these times accelerate and dynamize text, images, and processes, our artistic research practices require careful and situated reflection and accountability. Toolkits offer modular recipes, and using them carves out time and space, alongside the exhausting academic routines, for guided consideration and condition setting. Using a toolkit, one comes out with a plan of action. In artistic-research-supervision scenarios such a plan materializes as specific takes on inter- and intra-relating concepts, percepts, and affects, to borrow a tripartition from Gilles Deleuze and Félix Guattari.[2] Underlying this work and this publication is an attention to the question of how artistic and practice-based research relates or should relate to current societal and planetary urgencies. As Maria Hlavajova writes in the foreword, it is about *"practicing propositions* of what does not yet exist, [...] generative learning, as well as a prefigurative research space that involves collectively practicing a comprehensive and nuanced imagination about what ultimately makes for a good university."

Thus, *Challenging Institutionalization* is the outcome of collective knowledge production. For that constructive and inspiring exchange of thought we would like to thank all the contributors who entered into this collaboration with us, as well as all the participants in the 2023 summer school who came together and shared their practices and experiences. Finally, we would also like to thank the Novo Nordisk Foundation; Centre for Research in Artistic Practice at Aarhus University; The Royal Danish Academy of Fine Arts, School of Visual Arts; Utrecht University; and BAK, basis voor actuele kunst, Utrecht for making this project possible.

2. Gilles Deleuze and Félix Guattari, *What is Philosophy?*, trans. Hugh Tomlinson and Graham Burchell, European Perspectives (New York: Columbia University Press, [1991] 1994).

"F*CK YOU AND YOUR FOOTNOTES":
ON SOME TROPES IN THE RHETORICAL
SITUATION OF SUPERVISION.
Mick Wilson

[T]his is not a case of an inquiry extending to infinity.
That is, to find the best method of seeking the truth,
there is no need of another method for seeking the
method of seeking the truth, and there is no need of
a third method to seek the second method, and so
on to infinity. For in that way we should never arrive
at knowledge of the truth, or indeed at any knowledge.
The case is analogous to that of material tools,
where the same kind of argument could be employed.
To work iron, a hammer is needed, and to have a
hammer, it must be made. For this purpose there is
need of another hammer and other tools, and again
to get these there is need of other tools, and so on
to infinity. In this way one might try to prove, in vain,
that men have no power to work iron.

—Baruch Spinoza, *Tractatus de Intellectus Emendatione*, 1677[3]

Some Operational Assumptions
In order to rehearse a specific practice of supervising
doctoral research, it is necessary to set out something of the
operational assumptions that frame this teaching practice.
Firstly, and decisively, doctoral education is being approached
as an entry-level training in a craft of research. Even where
the student has an advanced practice, it is still a matter of
an entry-level training with respect to a craft of doing
research — I say "a" craft rather than "the" craft, as I am not
aware of a single all-encompassing craft of research, nor do I

3. Baruch Spinoza, *Tractatus de Intellectus Emendatione*, trans. Samuel Shirley, in
Spinoza: Complete Works, ed. Michael L. Morgan, (Indianapolis, IN, and Cambridge, MA:
Hackett, 2002), 9.

know of any research practitioner who convincingly advocates for such.

The model of research education proposed here is broadly that of many training programs in the arts, especially in the contemporary art field: a student learns and develops an artistic practice through actively "doing" such practice, while also looking at instances of contemporary art practice, and discussing in different idioms and rhetorical frames their own work and that of others, including that of their peers. In like manner, the doctoral student learns a craft of research by doing a research project or research process (i.e., a concrete and delimited instance of inquiry is undertaken as the occasion of acquiring a craft of doing research) and by discussing — in a range of specialist and nonspecialist idioms — the research undertakings of others.

While many art educations may seem to imagine themselves capable of supporting an unforeclosed and open spectrum of potential artistic practices, in contrast research educations — in most domains — tend to be a little less presumptive about their breadth of reach and capacity. They tend to specify their particular horizons of competency, their preferred thematic priorities, objects, instruments, methodologies, canons, concerns, and so forth.

Another key working assumption in this teaching practice pertains to the diverse domain of research that operates in some substantial way through practical production, art making, or forms of invention that are not primarily in the form of discursive textual inscription. In this approach to supervision, it is proposed to treat this congeries as divergent, plural, non-monolithic and in a state of flux. This avoids constructing an essential ontology of "practice-based research," "artistic research," "research creation," or similar, while accepting that such terms can be of use in different registers as designating nonessentialized typologies.

In this approach, saying that a research process is artistic is understood to be as helpfully informative about the nature, remit, tenor, and focus of the research as saying that it is done through French, or that it uses computers, or that it is done in the Netherlands, or that it often uses A4 sheets of paper, or that it is aural. This is not to say that specifying that artistic process or concerns are operative in a research undertaking is a nullity or trivial. It is just to say that it is far from exhaustively specifying the research and has relatively small value in disclosing what is at stake in a research undertaking or contribution. Denominating some inquiry as artistic research has only very limited utility in accessing the specificity of its contribution to a community of practice and knowledge. This is not to ignore the significance of institutional protocols, of constructing typologies, and of doing advocacy work. It is more a matter of placing these in a register that differs somewhat from that of the substantive research contribution circulating within given communities of knowledge/practice.

It is also important to note one further operating assumption here. In order to do research in the explicit and willed service of the process of learning a craft of research, it is necessary to specify a research task. Note that this is not necessarily a "project" but can take many forms, and may be a task that is in service to the research concerns and undertakings of others. Note also that this is not to say that all research must take the form of pursuing a prespecified research task. On the contrary, this is to be agnostic on the question of what might or might not be the fundamental requirement of research-in-general. It is rather to be committed on a pedagogical question of how to teach and how to learn a craft of research.[4]

4. This is to propose one viable model of learning a craft of research and not to suggest that this is the only possible route nor that there is only one model of doing research. I use the term "craft" loosely here to invoke the idea of an applied skill achieved by actively "doing." I am using it in the way that the older term *art* or the Latin *ars* or

It is important to qualify these working assumptions with the observation that artistic practices are not required to orient to a research paradigm or modality in order to have a claim on our attention. There are other indeed sometimes more interesting conversations to be had about contemporary art than the somewhat tired and often tendentious conversations about artistic research. Elsewhere, I have attempted to describe and advocate for a move away from what I term "a covering theory" of the specificity of artistic research or practice-based research, and for a move toward a focus on the concrete instances of inquiry and for the particularity of the research or knowledge work being done to be considered in tandem with the way it is being done.[5] In my own teaching, I try to minimize the use of covering pronouncements: "Art is basically X..." "Research is basically Y...." I only use these kinds of general formulations as a last—and unhappy—resort. There is a formulation of a language practice called English Prime, whereby speakers and writers are quarantined from the use of the verb "to be" and its variants. I propose to my students an analogous language practice of "research frugality" whereby researchers at the point of initiating and specifying a research project, for the purpose of learning a craft of research, forego the

Greek *technê* (τχνη) would have been used before the eighteenth-century elaboration of the system of fine arts and before the modern transformation in the usage of the terms *art* and *craft*. By speaking of *craft* I hope to indicate research as a practice that can be learned in a progressive manner, and learned primarily by doing research rather than by receiving descriptions of research or epistemological schemes. The latter have a central role but are not typically used as the primary means of entry into learning the activity. A friendly interlocutor might be tempted to ask at this point, "Well, if you are not going to specify what research-in-general is, then how can you specify what a research task is?" However, this is like saying, "Well, if you cannot tell us what the essence of nutrition is, how can you possibly decide what you would like to eat, taste, try to cook, or what might even make for a pleasant meal?" For all the glorious decades of rhizomatic enthusiasms, we sometimes seem to still grow along the fork-tongued paths of Aristotelian arboreal categories. Practical operations can be specified and pursued without initial dependency on the primacy of explicating conceptual schema or invoking foundational criteria. Furthermore the explication of any concept, the invoking of any criteria, will typically require operations that cannot be fully thematized in the same moment as these explanations and invocations are produced.

5. Mick Wilson, "Take One Step Forward, Two Steps Back," in *Futures of Artistic Research*, ed. Jan Kaila, Anita Seppä, and Henk Slager (Helsinki: Uniarts Helsinki, 2017).

use of general pronouncements on the nature, essence,
or fundamental criterion of art, of research, and of artistic
research and similar "covering" pronouncements, inasmuch as
this is practically possible.

This constraint is not proposed as a dogmatic prohibition,
but as a guide to writing and speaking that does not
easily avail itself of the generic covering pronouncement.
I recognize the need for generalization and summary in
description, conceptualization, and positioning. In what I have
already written here I have made use of generalizations
and summary descriptors. However, this use of summary
and generalization is not quite the same thing as the use of
covering pronouncements in formulating a specific research
undertaking, and it is the latter that is eschewed within
the research "frugality" proposed. The attempt is to avoid
using general covering pronouncements on the nature of
art, research, and artistic research in the formulation of a
concrete research task that is to be undertaken as a means
to learn a craft of research. What motivates this is the way
that such covering statements tend to reduce a nexus of
contestation to an unproblematizing statement of essence,
nature, or fundamental criterion and to the rehearsal of
cherished beliefs and rhetoric. Of course, this research
frugality is itself exquisitely vulnerable to this same critique.
However, I would hold out for the difference in operational
outcomes when we consider and apply all this within the space
of actual learning by doing, rather than exclusively within the
space of a textual inscription or a discursive exchange on
the general criterial or conceptual limits of key terms.

Of You and Yours
In adopting the title—"F*ck you and your footnotes":
On some tropes in the rhetorical situation of supervision"
—I am riffing on Lisa Soskolne's 2015 contribution to

PARSE Journal.[6] What interests me in this formulation, is the way a practice (the crit, or the critical apparatus of footnoting) is cast as a possession — "your crits" / "your footnotes." I describe this as the twinning of a persona ("you," the teacher, the supervisor, the police) and an institutional protocol ("your footnotes"). This twinning is proposed by a subject-in-refusal, who announces their refusal by disowning this practice — "Fuck you and your way of doing things: It is not what I stand for!"

This specific formulation — "F*ck you and your foot-notes" — is a fiction. However, let me share an example, derived from an email exchange with a doctoral researcher, that conforms to its general rhetorical form.

> I am deeply disturbed and disgusted by what you said in proposing an analogy between queer valorisation of transgression and alt-right shock tactics. I would like to have a one-to-one with you for clarification of your intentions in making your comments. I find that they reinforce a colonial hegemonic discourse that I am very much against. I find that it does not tend toward progressive knowledge. In fact, I find it rooted in white academic ideology.[7]

I am not so interested in the emotive tenor of this, so much as the operation of differentiation of "me" from "you" and "yours" — between "I" the subject in refusal and "you" the bearer of institutional protocol, of "hegemonic discourse." Let me take another example, which is also

6. Lise Soskolne, "You and Your Crits," *PARSE Journal*, no. 2 (2015), https://parsejournal.com/article/you-and-your-crits/.

7. I have adjusted the text to render my correspondent anonymous, while trying to retain the essential rhetorical form. The student is taking exception to the assertion that a queer advocacy of transgression as intrinsically good is vulnerable to infelicities or unhappy instantiations, when not anchored by some definitional or other mode of specification that delimits queer counter-hegemonic from what are effected as pro-hegemonic transgressive moves.

differentiating "me" and "you"—"me" in refusal and "you" as the bearer and agent of unacceptable institutional protocols.

I take this from the perennial return of the "academic writing" bogeyman: "Do you require me to produce an academic text?" Most of us working in doctoral education with artists can recount similar encounters and exchanges where a monstrous genre raises its dogmatic head summoning that fearful incantation of "the academic," as the spectre of the school rules, of the fearful "big other" arises from the deep to haunt the put-upon doctoral student. Supervisors are asked, as the friendly approachable neighborhood police, "Is this the law?" Here, without the combative aggression of my first example, is another instance of an operation in the speaker's positioning: "Is it the rule that *you* bear for *me*? I'm only asking *you* because I find academic writing can be very …." Dishearteningly, the much-maligned footnote —that most playful and potentially destabilizing of literary devices—is often adduced as the epitome of the *academic* and of its restrictive policing of mind, its injuring of potential and its denaturing of practice.

In focusing on the rhetorical dynamics of these conversational moves, I am especially interested in what the old rhetorical schools termed *ethos*. Ethos is, in one sense, the suasive effects of the speaker's character. It is the appeal to the speaker's character as the guarantor of reliable utterance: "Ask yourself, would I lie to you?" However, I am interested in the reverse engineering of this ethos. This is an interest not in the suasive power given to what I say by virtue of who I present myself to be, but rather in the production of my ethos, of my character, of my persona, by the very performance of my saying things.

In these two examples I cite, one of the processes unfolding is the production of "I"—of my ethos by a distanciation and differentiation, with respect to "you" and "yours."[8] Most importantly there is the address to "you" as the one who embodies institution, the one who is in, and of, the institution — invested — and serving as its police. We supervisors, that happy band of gaolers, blithely incarcerating our would-be runaways in the prison house of academic language practice.

Let me take a third example, which does not manifest with the explicit opposition of "me" and "you" but which I propose has a trace of the same rhetorical game, the same differential production of the speaker's *ethos*, as against that of the teacher who is cast as the bearer of institutional restriction and unfreedom.

> My wish to talk about a specific embodied experience is entangled with my uneasy and unresolved relationship with the tools provided by contemporary identity discussions and postcolonial/decolonial practices. On the one hand, I can fully relate to these discussions and practices. On the other hand, I find these are very restrictive and disallow a great deal. In a paradoxical manner, we end up defining ourselves through the very same systems of classification that we set out to deconstruct. In most situations, and especially academic situations, it is impossible to speak constructively about these contradictions.[9]

So here we have the "I" and "we" and the many "situations" that this "we" moves within. So why cast this as a case of an "I" and "you" where the teacher role is posited as the personification of institutional limitation and investment? I would argue that in this example it is the teacher and not the ambivalent PhD student who is placed as being most "especially" in the "academic situation," and that this is the primary

8. I say "one of the processes unfolding" because there is perhaps more afoot in these Oedipal games.

9. Again, I have adjusted to make this anonymous, but tried to retain the essential form.

positioning effect produced by the PhD student making this utterance.

Let me call upon one final example, which is the way in which PhD students by practice will sometimes appeal to a refusal of disclosure with respect to some aspects of their practice within the supervisory dialogue. There are lots of variations on this: "I don't want to displace the work itself by an explanation that will only overwrite and reduce the work"; "It's in the register of affect and performative force and not of semiosis or interpretation or through commentary that my practice is operating"; "It is in the doing not the saying." There is an especial interest for me in these formulas when they seek to refuse the requirement for a disclosure of a reasoning on "method." Some form of method talk is a typical requirement of doctoral pedagogy and examination, and is often seen by PhD students as an importuning, a putting-upon practice of an alien demand that risks spoiling and de-naturing it.[10]

10. In my teaching practice, I propose a simple distinction in word usage (at the commencement of studies) whereby "method" is employed as a term for naming a way of doing something, and "methodology" as a term for naming the reasoning and discursive unpacking of a way of doing something. This initial usage is then open for problematization at a later stage in the process. "Research method" is then a term for naming a way of doing inquiry. In some disciplines, there are very specific method resources in play such as. statistical analysis and inference, or construction of model organisms, or corpus analysis and so forth. Very often these method resources can also be used without being used in order to do research. A method—a way of working—can be opportune for doing an inquiry; it does not have to be something intrinsic to a work practice. For example, it is an affordance of interview practices that these can be used to do research, but it is not the intrinsic destiny of the device. Interviews can be done for entertainment or for assessment of suitability for employment. I labor these somewhat simple terminological usages, because there is so much misdirection in doctoral education arising from method talk. For this reason, within a supervision process, it helps to distinguish between different modes of method talk, most especially to distinguish between the fetish of "method-guarantee-ism"—a way of talking that suggests announcing possession of a method somehow guarantees the legitimacy of one's knowledge claims—and the pedagogical operation of "method-questioning"—a way of talking that asks, at certain moments in a process of learning to do something, why a particular way of way of proceeding or working has been adopted. The latter is a teaching action that is deemed useful only on certain occasions, and seen as enormously disruptive on others. It is in the inexact and exacting craft of teaching to judge the moment when such a question might be generative.

For the supervisor, addressed in this way — as the agent of the institutional imposition of unfreedom, as the diligent foot soldier frog-marching the student into imprisoning inscription within the system — there are a number of rhetorical moves possible. The supervisor/teacher might wish to evade the address by claiming to stand on the same side as the student, and disavow the "big other" and its institutional machinations, all those neoliberal devices, extractions and platitudes. "I also am a renegade, working below the radar, a refugee in the very same undercommons who disdains the siren call of the police, disdains the incitement to discourse, and refuses the heavy-handed regime of explanation." An alternate move is to play along and inhabit the role assigned by the student's mode of address, perhaps using it as an enabling move to concretize the "big other" for the student, who may need this figure as a foil and also need to play out the drama it allows. In this way, the supervisor reasserts, perhaps even tries to justify the institutional protocol contested by the student. Another move is to acquiesce in part to this address from the student, and then propose an inauthentic or *resistant* compliance: "Yes but let's just go along with this, and get what we want out of it without attracting too much attention and hassle." There is another deflationary move that rubs the other way and says, "Well let's, for a moment, put to one side all our critical, ideological, philosophical reservations and other cautions that we might have, and consider what is really being asked of us here. Perhaps, it's not quite so overdetermined and restrictive as it first appears." Another possibility is to ramp up the irritation and intensity at play in this game, by chasing after the cherished self-image of the student and attempt to rehearse an analysis with them of their speech act and its secret (or not so secret) animus. These are just some — not an exhaustive list — of the rhetorical move available to the teacher. They each afford something, and they each disable something, each can have some utility on some occasion, but all are somewhat unhappy moves, if only because they shore up business-as-usual as business-as-usual and leave one or more players happily ensconced in their un-self-critical image of their own critical reflexivity: unchallenged student, unchallenged teacher, and unchallenged institution.

Experiment in Speaking Differently

Recently, I have begun to experiment with a different rhetorical move. This is rather than directly contest or evade the mode of address within the student's utterance and its relative positioning of "me," "you," and the institutional protocol. It is to propose that "we" together reconstruct the exchange as one structured by a principle of inquiry.[11] This means instead of affirming our values, our perspectives, our respective positions, we try to bracket for a moment what we firmly believe and feel, and consider what we know and what we don't know within the situation we seem to be placed inside — or, indeed, to have electively entered. This is an attempt to recast the situation as a site and occasion of inquiry: What is it that is known and not quite known within the constellation of the operating situation? How might it be reframed as an act of inquiry rather than an act of affirming belief and position? Of course, beliefs, perspectives, positions are still at work in framing any inquiry. However, in this move to produce an ethos of inquiry rather than one of self-possession and confident pronouncement on "what I stand for," and on "how things really are" in the situation, a path to something unforeclosed may be opened.

This move may also be framed in terms of the frugality I mentioned earlier: This frugality that tries to minimize the

11. This rhetorical move invokes a provisional and highly fragile "we" inquirers in place of the certainties set to work in the foregoing oppositions of "me" against "you." It is of course a move that — like all invocations of the "we" — might easily become an oppressive power play and disciplinary imposition. However, it is not inevitable that it becomes so, and in the invocation of this "we" its provisional nature is foregrounded and remains subject to renegotiation or deconstruction as the process of inquiry proceeds.

appeal to covering pronouncements in specifying a research task. Frugality, as I am modelling it here, is a response to the question of how to negotiate the challenges of protracted onto-epistemological-cum-ethico-political disagreements, and of how to communicate from within that process of negotiation. It is especially a proposition of how to do this in a spirit of inquiry, rather than in the spirit of mastery and (complete) self-knowledge — "This is what I believe," "This is my embodied lived experience," "This is what I know in my heart," "This is what I am against," "This is where I'm coming from ...."

In this attempt at a rearticulation of the impasse, the questions proposed, the rhetorical moves are formed as follows: "What becomes possible if we pretend for a moment that we are not sure where we are coming from?" "What happens if we pretend for a moment that we do not fully accept our current mapping of positionality and institutional inscription?" "What might be allowed to unfold if we decide for a moment that our sense of our relative standing is not well specified nor fully known?"

This might seem to risk advocating some "view from nowhere" or some other "universalizing conceit" or to be yet another egregious action to disable and nullify difference, especially those differences subjected already to erasure and epistemic repression. Although of course there are many such potential risks for misstepping within this strategy, it is not necessary nor inevitable that this move to suspend "what I know for certain!" becomes one of repression and silencing. This proposed gambit is merely one moment, temporarily bracketed and not presented as a habitual or normative routine mode of operation. It is not the imposition of an epistemic principle or criteria of legitimacy, it is an elective and temporary experiment in thinking-speaking-doing otherwise, a heuristic play, not an appeal for guarantee.

In this move, we try to go back to the work of ethos, and specifically what might be called the "ethos of inquiry," meaning by this a willed disposition, an active "openness" to undergo a change of thinking, knowing, understanding, believing, positioning, or values, based on considered active participation and reflection on experience and encounter within a community of practice and dialogue.[12] The key feature of this ethos is a considered openness to the possibility of changing my mind, to the possibility of coming to think, believe, and act otherwise. Although I am attempting to outline the general operating terms of a practical strategy in supervision, this is still somewhat abstracted. So let me try to concertize it in relation to one of the earlier examples.

Say for instance the simple caution often expressed by some artist researchers — "I'm reluctant to talk about method, as this is not a way of talking integral to my practice. It is a model imposed from the humanities and sciences." Reconstructing this in a spirit of inquiry, with a certain frugality, would mean proposing a formulation something like: "Well, we suspect this might be the case, i.e., that this mode of disclosure harms or denatures that which is disclosed, and that it has its origins and mandates from elsewhere. However, on what basis do we suspect or know this?" "With what different possible agendas might such method talk be framed?" "What are the possible genealogies of method talk?" "Let's test — with respect to a concrete instance — and seek to describe the affordances and disablements of this method talk."

An important aspect of this move will be that on occasion — responsive to whatever particular issues might have been set in play — the question of institution will be

12. The "ethos of inquiry" is a term the construction and justification for which I can only summarily indicate here. An early attempt at elaborating the term can be found in Mick Wilson, "Between Apparatus and Ethos: On Building a Research Pedagogy in the Arts," in *Artists with PhDs: On the New Doctoral Degree in Studio Art*, ed. James Elkins (Washington: New Academia, 2014).

activated, but activated as a matter of inquiry and not simply as the already known. This is not then the institution as already specified in various traditions of institutional critique or analyses of neoliberal reforms and proxy markets etc., but rather the institution as an object of inquiry, not an essence already disclosed and foreclosed in advance. However, it is also not the institution simply taken at its word, and accepted in its own self-assertion and announcement.[13]

This is a horizon of inquiry that allows the possibility of new rhetorical situations to be rehearsed and invented which are not the tired drama of "me," "you" and the institutional protocol that you force upon me, not the tired drama that requires me to declare that I take exception to this rule.[14] Let me be clear, though, I am not proposing that a simple rearrangement of rhetorical devices is sufficient to produce massively transformative effects. However, I am proposing that the current tendencies for the recycling and repetition of these familiar tropes is a fundamental blockage in developing a craft of inquiry.

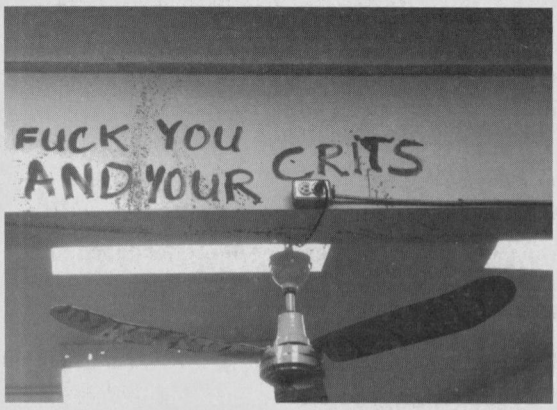

13. I think this kind of move will be especially helpful in avoiding the empirically vacant and astonishingly reductive thinking at work in the diagnosis of artistic research as a reflex of Bologna reforms or of cognitive capital.

14. Perhaps what is being especially obscured in the recycling of these tropes is our deficit of understanding with respect to the institutions we inhabit, appropriate, and reproduce, and perhaps even that capacity we have to invent and re-instantiate.

MAKING CONTRIBUTIONS
Laura Guy

Contribution is a condition of participation at the summer school, with the days structured around short presentations made by all attendees. These presentations on the subject of supervising practice research do not simply sit alongside a pre-determined curriculum. Our contributions *make* the curriculum, offering material for group discussion and further inquiry.

Contribution is also a condition that all doctoral work is required to meet if it is to be successful. Looking up the regulations for the Degree of Doctor of Philosophy at the art school where I work, I read that a candidate is required to make "a significant and original contribution to existing knowledge." In the UK, the extent to which this condition has been met is interrogated during the viva, an oral examination on which the outcome of the award depends.

Although contribution is a dictate of all kinds of doctoral work, the need to quantify or qualify exerts specific pressures on PhDs by creative practice. In an essay examining the issue of evidencing knowledge production within practice, Michael Cawood Green and Tony Williams suggest of the UK context that the onus placed on text to do this work of evidencing is challenging, if not completely disorientating, to visual and creative outputs. They write:

> We would like to talk about distortion—the likelihood that "writing up" reflection on practice into the classic scholarly article is likely to distort practice, like a strangely shaped mirror in a hall of mirrors, making some areas of the body bulge and others thin to almost nothing.[15]

15. Michael Cawood Green and Tony Williams, "On Reflection: The Role, Mode and Medium of the Reflective Component in Practice as Research," *TEXT* 22, no. 1 (2018), https://doi.org/https://doi.org/10.52086/001c.25106.

The authors acknowledge that this is not a new problematic even if it is a stubborn one. Within the UK model, text continues to be asserted as the privileged medium through which research findings might be evidenced and claims made.

Though the authors suggest several useful approaches to counter this, other hierarchies of value are at work within and around PhDs by creative practice. Emphasis is unevenly distributed across the phrasing "a significant and original contribution to existing knowledge." Supplementing contribution, originality stresses proprietary as much as participation. This is inflected by the various checks and balances through which value is measured in research.

As I write this short text in early 2024, major changes are proposed to the way that funding for doctoral study is organized in the UK. These changes coincide with —indeed are a route to implement—further defunding by the state of the arts and humanities. As part of the proposed changes, the number of overall PhDs funded by the Arts and Humanities Council (AHRC) is anticipated to be cut by a quarter by 2029–30.[16]

This reduction in resource is also a redistribution and reorganization of funding. These changes indicate a move toward strategic investment that will be focused around par-ticular research themes. At the time of writing these include the creative economy and "humanities for a healthy planet, people and place," a vague designation that incorporates themes with scientific inflection such as ecological approaches both to public health and wellness and to climate change.

Creative practice has much to offer these urgent areas of inquiry, yet the orientation of doctoral funding toward centrally devised, governmentally driven, strategic investment belies the ongoing and ideologically motivated attack upon

16. Jack Grove, "Arts and Humanities Research Council Cuts Funded PhDs by Quarter," *Times Higher Education*, September 10, 2023, https://www.timeshighereducation.com/news/arts-and-humanities-research-council-cuts-funded-phds-quarter.

the arts and humanities in higher education enacted by successive governments. The measure of value for public money is largely determined by economic benefit for society and rests on an instrumentalized notion of contribution within research. It is couched in the language of innovation that pervades UK research and its indicators of value.

Writing on the Better Shelter project, a product and campaign launched by IKEA and the United Nations High Commissioner Office, Ariella Aïsha Azoulay identifies the "racist capitalist economy of innovation and partnership between corporations, built upon the creation of displaced clients of the humanitarian industry that provides them with 'innovative products.'"[17] The brief critique of innovation that Azoulay offers is precise, an entry point for problematizing the orientation of the human within rights-based discourse in a study that seeks to unlearn the legacy and affects of imperialism. The project from which this excerpt is taken was at least partly prompted by Azoulay's experience working within the neoliberal university. She directs us to stakes of resisting contribution as either a proprietorial claim or as one delivered within a client-based model, especially when made from institutions shaped by imperialism and its legacies.

At present, many thinkers are interested in re-examining the value of productivity in our time of crises. In *The Plague*, British psychoanalyst Jacqueline Rose's astonishing treatise addressing the aftermath of COVID-19, the author argues that "if we want to prepare for a better, fairer, life—if we want to prepare for any kind of future at all—we must slow the pace and change our relationship to time."[18] The theatre and performance scholar Carl Lavery proposes an ecological approach to participation that

17. Ariella Aïsha Azoulay, *Potential History: Unlearning Imperialism* (London: Verso, 2019), 449.
18. Jacqueline Rose, *The Plague* (London: Fitzcarraldo, 2023), 85.

does not revolve around issues of intentionality and
agency; rather, it concerns an aesthetics of disclosure.
In other words, the point is not to produce yet more
artworks that seek to create participation or immersion
(or both) as intentional acts; rather the more humble,
but just as vital, objective is to uncover the extent to
which we are already participating, always already
immersed.[19]

Artist Maria Howard works in a studio two floors beneath
my office at the art school, making modest sculptures from
unfired clay. Her PhD research interrogates the architectural
column, a feature of classical architecture incorporated widely
within colonial architectural styles. As well as a building, we
also share a city — Glasgow — that was once described as
the "second city of the Empire." Howard's work starts here
and works out from urban sites encountered in various states
of dilapidation, many of which feature neoclassical elements
such as columns.

Howard's ceramics are small in scale and fragile,
objects made by hand from parian, a fine, unglazed porcelain.
A recent series of column-like forms are cast from the
stout stems of giant hogweed. This invasive and poisonous
species that "colonizes" riverbanks was first introduced to
Britain as an ornamental plant in the early nineteenth century.
Its striated form is as entangled in histories of imperialism
as the architectural features it resembles.

In Howard's objects, and the creative writing that
she produces alongside them, columns are encountered
everywhere throughout the city. Sometimes they are
decorative. Other times they are integral to the structures
they support. Remapping these structures along with various
root systems that threaten to overwhelm them, Howard

19. Carl Lavery, "Participation, Ecology, Cosmos," in *Reframing Immersive Theatre: The Politics and Pragmatics of Participatory Performance*, ed. James Frieze (London: Palgrave Macmillan, 2016), 304.

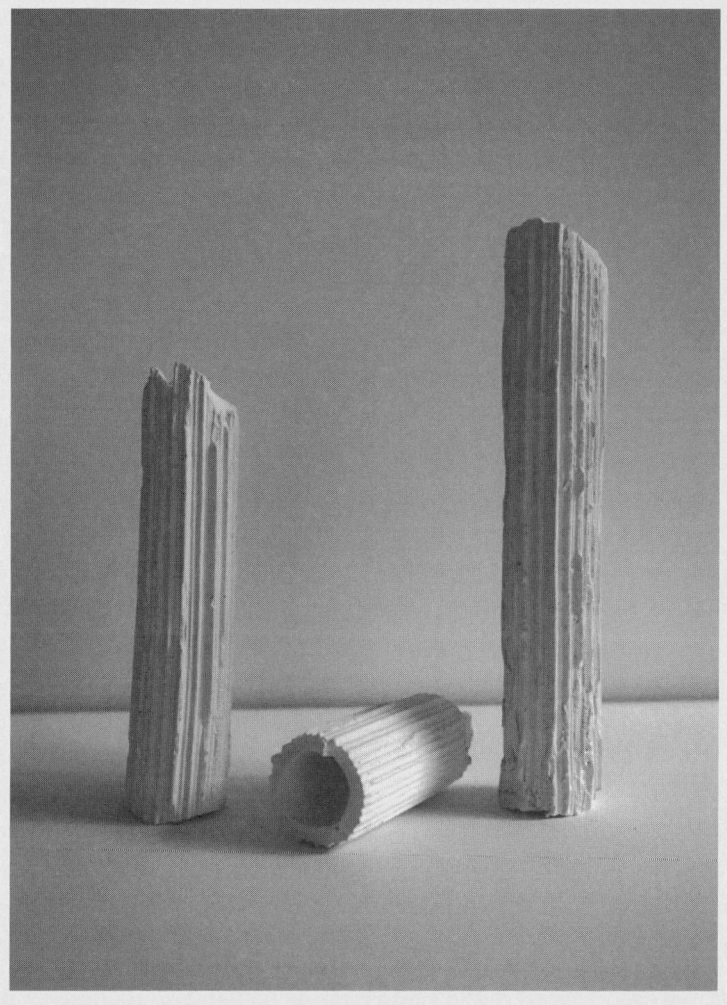

Maria Howard, *column as invasive species*, 2024, unfired parian clay, dimensions variable (max 25 cm)

interrogates complex ecologies that bind us into post-industrial and post-colonial formations.

Sharing an institution, and working close to hand, Howard's sculptures help me to think through what an ecology of contribution in practice research might offer. Instead of asserting a proprietorial claim to knowing, contribution implies a relationality that is always already a part of the process of making.

LOST LUGGAGE
Maureen de Jager

Limbo

I arrived at a loss (as the saying goes)—with my luggage in
limbo, somewhere between Johannesburg and Amsterdam.
I was minus clean clothes; minus my familiar things; minus a
handcrafted artist's book, which I had tossed into my suitcase
almost as an afterthought. Titled *WRITING (AS) PASSAGE*,
my bookwork comprised passages of text excerpted from
my PhD thesis and transcribed, by hand, onto the cut-up test
prints from an earlier project. A meditation (of sorts)
on practice-based writing as a rite of passage, *WRITING
(AS) PASSAGE* had seemingly failed to make "safe passage"
(it was *lost*, and, as I settled into this unhappy realization,
so indeed was I).

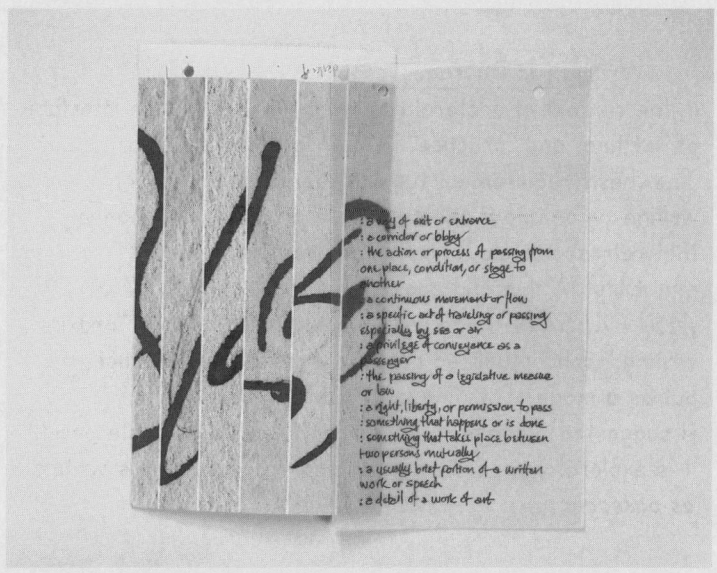

Maureen de Jager, *WRITING (AS) PASSAGE* (2023), page 22.
Test print with handwritten text on tracing paper overlay.

Passage

noun

: a way of exit or entrance
: a corridor or lobby
: the action or process of passing from one place, condition, or stage to another
: a continuous movement or flow
: a specific act of traveling or passing especially by sea or air
: a privilege of conveyance as a passenger
: the passing of a legislative measure or law
: a right, liberty, or permission to pass
: something that happens or is done
: something that takes place between two persons mutually
: a usually brief portion of a written work or speech
: a detail of a work of art

verb

: to go past or across
: to subject to passage[20]

Writing (as Passage)

In the context of doctoral research in the arts, the interface of "writing" and "practice" is often a site of tension. The thesis requirement typically demands a body of writing *on* or *about* one's creative practice, in a manner that retrospectively "locks down" its open-ended mutability. Within and against this tension, *WRITING (AS) PASSAGE* tentatively posited the notion of "praxis-writing," conceptualized not as the inverse of practice, but as a mode of writing *as* practice. Praxis-writing (I suggested) uses modalities of practice to elucidate practice. It is exploratory, performative, and processual; it is writing *as passage*.

20. "Passage," Merriam-Webster, accessed January 25, 2024, https://www.merriam-webster.com/dictionary/passage.

To think of writing *as passage* (as *a* passage) is to recognize the inherent restlessness of writing, which always gestures beyond itself. "Passage" implies a motion into/out of/between/across: "a way of exit or entrance," "the action or process of passing," "a continuous movement or flow."[21] For Janneke Adema, the book (or text) is always caught up in "a process of becoming (albeit one that is continuously interrupted and disturbed)."[22] This is because books (or texts or pieces of writing) are "performative; they are reality-shaping, not just mirroring of objective knowledge."[23]

In this same vein, praxis-writing embraces the "reality-shaping" impetus of its intrinsic performativity. Instead of closing in *on* practice (as a reductive framing/exegesis) it opens up *as* practice, in a manner that is, to use Jill Bennett's expression, "generative rather than representational."[24] In line with the practice that it elucidates (albeit obliquely), praxis-writing directs itself at "a not knowing, or a not-yet-knowing"; it "creates room for that which is unthought, that which is unexpected—the idea that all things could be different."[25]

Beginning to Know

To write on praxis *as praxis* is thus the challenge; to write *as a matter of praxis* ... Sometimes—oftentimes—I write to *work out*, in the handling of language, what it is that I could be thinking. And it is in these moments (as I weigh up my words, pressing them into the palm of my hand) that I begin to know.[26]

21. "Passage."
22. Janneke Adema, *Living Books: Experiments in the Posthumanities* (Cambridge, MA: MIT Press, 2021), 248.
23. Adema, *Living Books*, 20.
24. Jill Bennett, *Practical Aesthetics: Events, Affects and Art after 9/11* (London: Tauris, 2012), 153.
25. Henk Borgdorff, "The Production of Knowledge in Artistic Research," in *The Routledge Companion to Research in the Arts*, ed. Michael Biggs and Henrik Karlsson (London: Routledge, 2010), 61.
26. Text excerpted from Maureen de Jager, *WRITING (AS) PASSAGE* (2023).

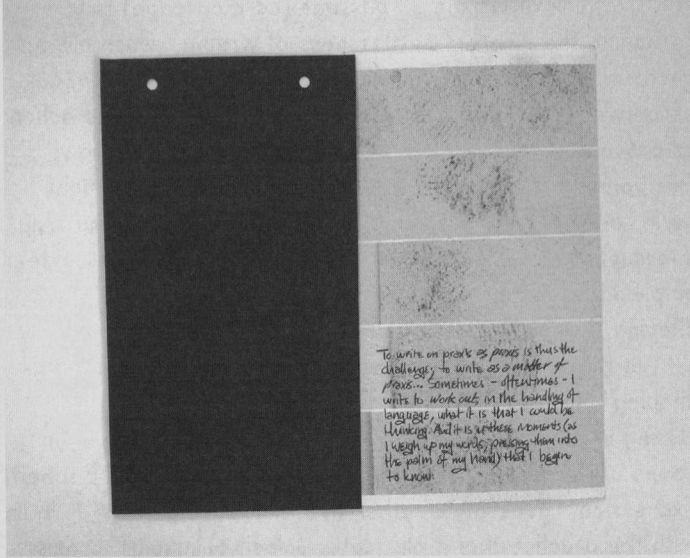

Maureen de Jager, *WRITING (AS) PASSAGE* (2023), page 27.
Test print with handwritten text on carbon paper overlay.

The World to Come

Praxis-writing (as *praxis*) is "always in part the creation of the world to come,"[27] exemplifying "the critical and inextricable meld of theory and practice."[28] How, then, does one supervise a doctoral student in and through this liminal space, the "becoming," "not-yet-knowing" and "beginning to know?" For, in this scenario, "writing up" is no longer a retrospective "explanation" of practice (as if this were stable and concluded) but a perpetual and prospective "writing through and throughout."

Barbara Bolt's notion of "praxical engagement — which emphasizes the ongoing "work" of art on makers and readers

27. John Lysaker, "Writing as Praxis," *The Journal of Speculative Philosophy* 28, no. 4 (2014): 535, https://doi.org/10.5325/jspecphil.28.4.0521.
28. Robyn Stewart, "Practice vs Praxis: Constructing Models for Practitioner-Based Research," *TEXT* 5, no. 2 (2001): 3, https://doi.org/https://doi.org/10.52086/001c.35795.

—is perhaps useful in this regard." [29] The "work" of art lies partly in the student's intrepid engagement with praxis, as an exploratory "knowing through handling." But the research process also includes the reciprocal workings *of* praxis *on* the student-researcher, in a manner supported by the "work" of supervision. As Angelique Bletsas explains, producing a thesis entails not only the completion of a finite text but also "the constitution of the PhD student as a discoursing subject"—it is a *rite of passage*, in other words. [30]

Against this backdrop, the supervisor's role is (arguably) to *facilitate passage*, or even "to subject to passage," as the need arises. [31] At times, the student may face the passage of praxis-research with trepidation and distrust, preferring certitude and stasis over limbo. At times, the student may accept (and even embrace) the passage as a "privilege of conveyance" [32]—appreciating, in turn, the supervisor's role as "conveyancer." Eventually, hopefully, the student may come to understand that praxis-supervision is its own form of passage, as "something that takes place between two [or more] persons mutually." [33]

Arrival

I arrived at a loss (as the saying goes), temporarily unmoored by the interrupted passage of my luggage (my familiar things; my bookwork). As it transpired, my bookwork was *not* irretrievably lost. For several days, it lay mute and unopened in a dank back room at baggage reclaim (nestled in a protective bed of compressed clothes, in a hard-shell suitcase, in the dark). *WRITING (AS) PASSAGE* survived the passage home (still mute and unopened), a meditation on

29. Barbara Bolt, *Art Beyond Representation: The Performative Power of the Image* (London: I.B. Tauris, 2004), 65.

30. Angelique Bletsas, "The PhD Thesis as 'Text': A Post-Structuralist Encounter with the Limits of Discourse," *New Scholar* 1, no. 1 (2011): 9.

31. "Passage," Meriam-Webster.

32. "Passage."

33. "Passage."

praxis-writing that mattered in passing (appropriately so). Its rereading, all these months later, now enables passage into a liminal space of reflection: a brief passage *on* passage, "a way of [both] exit [and] entrance," and finally, simply, "something that happens or is done."[34]

34. "Passage."

EXCEPTIONAL US
Andrea Philips

Within any generic argument about education's capitalization, or the meritocratic ascendency warranted by a practice-based PhD; beyond the circularity of calls for artistic entry into, then rejection of, the "higher" academy, lies a continuously denied repetition of the production of exceptionalism.

Carl Schmitt designated a state of exception as that which occurs when a sovereign (or someone determined to assert their sovereignty) takes the law into their own hands, bypassing juridical—"democratic"—legislation. From democracy (the artist demands their rights to the self-determination of the shape and form of their PhD) to exceptionalism (the artist refuses the regulations of the PhD on the basis of their difference), the artist-researcher, like the market in which their subject is conditioned, must negotiate how to be exceptional to governance frameworks. A savior of critical research practice, or an autocrat perfecting self-mastery? The institution lags behind, afraid of its own market redundancy, rendered speechless through the fog of bureaucracy. The supervisor, an implement, plays back and forth.

1

Where can the work of (re)creative thinking be done in the midst of the enclosure of the art world, in the vocational enclosure of the university, in the ideological enclosure that one might call, even though both of its terms need radically to be called into question, the intellectual's public?[35]

35. Fred Moten, *Black and Blur: Consent not to Be a Single Being* (Durham, NC: Duke University Press, 2017), 155.

It is perhaps self-evident that the field of higher degrees, particularly as it has been developed as a mechanism of exclusion (economic, racial, gendered), has deep roots in our colloquial understanding of what it is to be exceptional. For example, it is presumed that the field of PhD research is only a field for those that have attained an exceptional form of proven intelligence; that that form of intelligence meets criteria that are regulated through academic histories of sanctioned knowledge; that those that name the exception are in themselves exceptional; that the infrastructural systematization of exceptionality is itself sanctioned by the preclusive strata of the social as they exist in a first world modernist epistemology.

This book addresses the ways in which practice-based (or "artistic") PhD supervision is provided and supported in — largely — Northern European art schools and includes contributions from both supervisors (such as myself) and practice-based researchers, and it is focused on practice in the arts. While I recognize the generic nature of exceptionalism within the race, class, and gendered mechanisms of higher education, here I want to point to a specific, and logically contorted, aspect of exceptionalism at work in practice-based PhDs in the arts. My contribution will, therefore, speak from within an already delimited problematic to which the practice-based PhD is indebted, and in full acknowledgement of the history of practice/theory debates that still cause tension in this field (despite their longevity) as well as the pugnacity often enacted to defend its externally presumed coherence. I want to examine this coherence as it pertains to the already acknowledged contradictions inherent within practice-based research, namely, how can practice be assessed as knowledge production? Why does practice need a theoretical addendum to prove it is knowledge? How can practice-based PhDs be supervised? Etc. Such navel gazing seeks a coherent face for a field. Why? What does this teleological demand do for research itself?

2

The supervisor, an implement, plays back and forth. When
Fred Moten says, "Where can the work of (re)creative
thinking be done in the midst of the enclosure of the art
world, in the vocational enclosure of the university, in the
ideological enclosure that one might call, even though both
of its terms need radically to be called into question, the intellectual's public?" he calls into question the cycles of power
as they are enacted through structures of teaching *to*,
teaching *about*, teaching *what it means* to be an intellectual,
separated from a public, whose public is, somehow, *owned*
by the researcher. This *owned* is what the supervisor confers
in a strict sense: the right to have a *public*, the distinction,
the exception.

It is, thus, inferred, or presumed, or expected, that
the supervisor knows how to correlate an *owned*, the having
of a vocation; to pass on the legitimizing claim of a *mine*:
my knowledge, my art, my public. They are an implement
of passage, a conduit of the exception.

I will return to the supervisor; the vocation, its construction. As will become clear, my central criticism of the conditions of knowledge production generally, but also particularly
in the context of practice-based research, is this construction
of a vocation that is both separate and separating from
other knowledges and practices that are largely unrecognized.
The supervisor, in a bare reading, is the person that trains
up the builder of vocational barriers — or enclosures as Moten
says. So, in what follows, the supervisor's role as a builder
of barriers haunts my thoughts. I think there is another
way of supervising, a way of admitting the joyful inadequacy,
the generous permeability of thinking and acting. I will call
this "good enough" supervising.

3

In my experience, over the past twenty years there has been a notable shift in the ambitions of the people, be their artists, musicians, theater makers, dramatists, etc., that pursue practice-based PhDs. When I first started supervising in the Department of Art at Goldsmiths in the early 2000s those people that I supervised were in the main, for example, artists who are painting and writing about the history of figuration, or musicians performing and at the same time looking into the history of improvisation. These examples are perhaps slightly exaggerated, but the practice-based PhD opened up forms of intelligibility for these people that were otherwise occlusive. It enabled practitioners to contribute to the formations of knowledge within the university (to become authors, "poets of their own affairs").[36] It conferred power where it was assumed there was none. It presumed a lack. It made the supposed powerlessness of art into an idiom of power in order that it might compete with other subjects and subject positions, whilst retaining its right of mute difference. This relation between lack and muteness is a problem which contemporary structures of practice-based research inherit and usually progress.[37]

Over the course of my twenty-year experience as a supervisor, while the exacerbations of mute lack continue, I have also seen the area of academic training, knowledge-gathering and examination transformed by both the positions of people who are engaging in practice-based PhD research, and the positions of people that are supervising them.

36. Michel de Certeau, *The Practice of Everyday Life* (Berkeley: University of California Press, 1984), 34.

37. Another paper must recognize the inherent racialization (Moten's "deprivation-in-privilege") that is missing from my argument here. The terms "mute" and "lack" are references inverted for their ostensible deprivilegization. This could be read as a serious mistake. See Denise Ferreira da Silva, *Unpayable Debt* (London: Sternberg Press, 2022) for a poethics of unpayability with an extremely different politics of lack.

In particular, the discursive arena of practice has been absolutely changed by the entry of the "social turn" into its field, influenced by forms of knowledge produced within the wider social sciences from which it borrows much methodology and content, alongside a newly enacted claim for difference from or to this wider field continues. What Moten calls for "(re)creative thinking" to "be done in the midst of the enclosure of the art world," many would respond that this is already at work in the arena of social practice PhDs (by which I mean artists engaging in forms of nominally collaborative, ethnographic, participatory, or action research that propose a breaking out of the enclosures of the art world by dint of the ethics of contact). I have attempted to unpick the problems of these categories and practices elsewhere.[38] Aside from the multiplications of the assumptions of mute/ lack that govern many of these practices (the artist does not have to speak/the participants speak on their behalf/ the participants are a lack that is fulfilled by the art), the university has been obliged to deal with the ethics of its own handling of knowledge culled from elsewhere (in other words, the complexities indicated in Moten's "vocational" enclosure).

> What comes before autonomy must, then, also *exceed* it, that is to say, succeed it, survive it, and indefinitely overrun it.[39]

But my contribution is not about practice-based research and the social turn (despite the need for an intricate, detailed and as yet unwritten political study of the topic), but an acknowledgement that many of my conclusions are influenced by the contradictions of study, power, and exceptionality

38. See, for example, Andrea Phillips, "Arts Organisations, Educational Institutions and the Collaborative Imperative," in *Institution as Praxis: New Curatorial Directions for Collaborative Research*, ed. Carolina Rito and Bill Balaskas (Berlin: Sternberg Press, 2020).

39. Jacques Derrida, *Politics of Friendship* (London: Verso, 1997), 365.

that become hypervisible in such projects (that autonomy, structured into the telos of a project, that, in Derrida's words, denies the "symmetrical and heteronomical curvature of the social space prior to any organized *socius*").[40] Rather than profoundly changing our understanding of the subject of research alongside the subjectivity of the researcher, I notice an entrenching of a form of isolationism within practice-based research, especially that with a social claim: to not be the social as a cause of study even as sociality is the aesthetic regime. Superficially this is due to accusations of "the academicization of art" occasionally emitted by art stylists; more pertinently, it is to do with the artist-researchers' educated instinct that the mute/lack has been inculcated into their chosen life, and while muteness serves a purpose, lack cannot be filled by the speech of others whilst autonomy is necessitated.

To claim exception — difference from the norm — in research, to aim beyond the academy (towards the public or the world) is, rather than revolutionary, exactly the way modernity has always demanded the university should operate (the foundation, in fact). Revolution — perhaps via the establishment of equity within the institution — is an excellent goal, but one that is hindered by the self-imposed demands that being a client of the intellectual machine imposes. Clientage — an ambivalent dependency — within the economic and aesthetic infrastructure of the institution struggles to maintain a psychosomatic isolation in the name of consumer rights ("I am paying to be better than others"). The supervisor is the conduit. This is further enforced when exceptionalism and clientage meet, in the conductive body of the producer (in this case the supervisor), constructing a toxic habitus wherein all research must be economized, and in which all higher education institutions must become porous to the externalities that they have traditionally been

40. Derrida, *365*.

exceptionalized from (a double exception). Bourdieu would remind us that all habiti are more or less toxic; that the fact of the existence of a habitus is the always already circulation of the condition: "To speak of habitus is to include in the object the knowledge which the agents, who are part of the object, have of the object, and the contribution this knowledge makes to the reality of the object."[41]

4

What is exception? Beyond colloquial uses (to stand out as much better than competitors, to be beyond normative forms of excellence, to be distinct, etc.), the concept has a specific history grounded in legal theory in which was determined both the power of rule and those deemed to life outside of regulation (outcast or existing outside regulated social structure).

Twentieth-century political-philosophical history moved exceptionalism from a political and juridical question stemming from Roman law towards an ethico-juridical tool to challenge what it means to "live politically." Giorgio Agamben begins *State of Exception* by saying:

> There is still no theory of the state of exception in public law, and jurists and theorists of public law seem to regard the problem more as a *quaestio facti* [question of fact] than as a genuine juridical problem. Not only is such a theory deemed illegitimate by those authors who affirm that the state of necessity, on which the exception is founded, cannot have a juridical form, but it is difficult even to arrive at a definition of the term given its position at the limit between politics and law.[42]

41. Pierre Bourdieu, *Distinction: A Social Critique of the Judgement of Taste* (Cambridge, MA: Harvard University Press, 1979), 467.
42. Giorgio Agamben, *State of Exception* (Chicago: University of Chicago Press, 2005), 1.

Agamben here insists on a legal—and perhaps ethical—
ambiguity regarding what the exception is (an ambiguity
that he goes on the expand). He quotes the legal and
political theorist Carl Schmitt, who begins his 1922 essay
Political Theology with, "Sovereign is he who decides on
the exception."[43] This phrase, much picked over in the
century that follows, is normally read through the fact that
Schmitt joined the National Socialist party in Germany in
1932. Schmitt directs the reader to understand that the
sovereign (the ruler of any constitutional or nonconstitutional
state), when confronted with a "state of exception"
("any kind of severe economic or political disturbance that
requires the application of extraordinary measures") has the
right to override constitutional regulations in order to declare
a person/people/situation/event outside the constitution.[44]
Beyond declaring that thing unconstitutional, that thing is
beyond the field of constitutional practice. Deemed thus, the
thing is available to the sovereign to do with as they please.
For Schmitt, who in 1933 was quick to join in with Nazi book
burning, this power—to name or designate the exception—
is the very power that constitutes sovereignty. In Schmitt's
1932 publication *The Concept of the Political* he clarifies his
position: "The specific political distinction to which political
actions and motives can be reduced is that between friend
and enemy."[45] For Levinas, and, as has been referenced,
Derrida, this very notion constitutes the basis of what it
means to be other or othered, the basis of which opens up
the thing to direct spatial, physical, and psychological violence.
Schmitt says, "The exception is to be understood to refer
to a general concept in the theory of the state, and not
merely as a construct applied to any emergency decree or

43. Carl Schmitt, *Political Theology: Four Chapters on the Concept of Sovereignty*
(Chicago: University of Chicago Press, 2005), 5.
44. Schmitt, *Political Theology*, 5n1.
45. Carl Schmitt, *The Concept of the Political* (Chicago, IL: University of Chicago
Press, 1996), 26.

state of siege." In other words, it is the exception that gathers the sovereign to itself.[46]

Here, the sovereign (the ruler or that person who has taken rule), in a state of emergency, is able to transcend state constitutionalism — the rule of law — for what they deem to be the public good (which might be the meting out of extreme violence to annihilate the exception). The exception is thus a figure/thing that in its obverse constitutes — shapes, performs — sovereign-controlled concepts of the so-called good and the constitution of the so-called public.

Agamben's *Homo Sacer: Sovereign Power and Bare Life* (1995) is both a retort to Schmitt and a complication of the political-conceptual forms of both the sovereign and the exception. In it he reminds us of the Ancient Greek distinction between *zoe* and *bios*. He says:

> The Greeks had no single term to express what we mean by the word "life." They used two terms that, although traceable to a common etymological root, are semantically and morphologically distinct: *zoe*, which expressed the simple fact of living common to all living beings (animals, men, or gods), and *bios*, which indicated the form or way of living proper to an individual or a group.[47]

Homo Sacer (in Roman law literally: set apart from the socius, and both hallowed and cursed) is a person who is banned and might be killed by anybody, but must not be sacrificed in a religious ritual. It is the state of exception. "The protagonist of this book is bare life," Agamben says, continuing; "that is, the life of *homo sacer* (sacred man), who *may be killed and yet not sacrificed*, and whose essential function in modern politics we intend to assert."[48]

46. Schmitt, *Political Theology*, 5.
47. Giorgio Agamben, *Homo Sacer: Sovereign Power and Bare Life* (Stanford, CA: Stanford University Press, 1995), 9.
48. Agamben, 12.

Bare life, therefore, is not simply zoe (living outside or beyond the law), but a form of being bound to it whilst excluded from it through the form of sacrilege which both suspends and binds close the individual to the category of "exclusion/inclusion." The thing "separates and opposes himself to his own bare life and, at the same time, maintains himself in relation to that bare life in an inclusive exclusion."[49] Derrida takes up this friend/enemy, inclusion/exclusion thesis in *The Politics of Friendship* when he claims that justice — nonjuridical — beyond the dualism of zoe/bios, takes the form of an "infinite place of resistance." A place that, however, despite its infinity, is primarily resistant to immanence. Of which, the philosophical scholar Arianne Conty asks, "How can the citizen be bound by fraternity and community and vow to protect the nation, while professing at the same time a radical universal freedom and equality that has no borders?"[50] This idea of justice that supersedes a Schmittian idea of the state and the sovereign leaves recipients in a difficult position: the phenomenological metaphysics of infinite justice, inflected with expanded notions of non-teleological belief that is at the same time anti-immanent (since there is no teleology) suspends the friend/enemy in an exceptionalism which is both sovereign (non-immanent) and anti-sovereign (infinite).

5

The claim of many practice-based scholars is that practice-based research is exceptional and cannot be treated (organized, supervised, examined, assessed) in the same way as non-practice PhDs. Beyond the general exceptionalism of the PhD form with which I began, *this* exceptionalism is based on what are in my view Jacques Rancière's deeply

49. Agamben, 12.
50. Arianne Françoise Conty, "Sovereign Power, Sovereign Justice: Carl Schmitt and Jacques Derrida on the State of Exception," *Philosophy Today* 62, no. 3 (2018): 3, https://doi.org/10.5840/philtoday20181024229.

critical idea of the aesthetic regime of art, in which art "frees
itself from any specific rule, from any hierarchy of the arts,
subject matter, and genres."[51] This it does "by destroying the
mimetic barrier that distinguished doing and making affiliated
with art from other ways of doing and making, a barrier that
separated its rules from the order of social occupation."[52]
In a double move, Rancière thus disaffiliates art (art in/of the
aesthetic regime — a regime that is not tethered to historical
or genre or material designation) from both representative
chronology and political ("ethical") injunction. It is this form
of exceptionalism that both now "makes" art and frees it
from hierarchies of necessity. Rancière's description is
both accurate and acute; it also leaves the practice-based
researcher with a new power: total subjective designation.
If we push this claim through the sieve of Schmitt/Agamben/
Derrida/Rancière outlined previously we might reach some
initial conclusions:

a. Schmitt:
   – Practice serves the sovereign by designating the
   juridical limit;
   – Practice is the exception due to its acting outside
   of sovereignty.

b. Derrida:
   – Practice/the practitioner performs nonjuridical justice;
   – Practice takes/makes the form of an "infinite place
   of resistance."

c. Agamben:
   – Is the practitioner *homo sacer* (who *may be killed and
   yet not sacrificed*)?

51. Jacques Rancière, *The Politics of Aesthetics: The Distribution of the Sensible*
(London: Continuum, 2004), 23.
    52. Rancière, 23.

d. Rancière:
  – Art made by the practitioner in the aesthetic regime
  is free from representation and ethics and can thus take
  any position.

It is in this miasma of definitions that the very theorists so
enmeshed/utilized in critical and political-art discourse provide
the perfect conditions for presumptions about the nature of
practice-based PhDs:

  1. The *normal* PhD is regulated by a state constitution
  that is questioned by practice;
  2. Practice is assumed to be exceptional due to its
  immanent/incalculable nature (if it meets the criteria of
  the aesthetic regime);
  3. But practice is also sovereign: it overrides the
  constitution and declares that it is itself the exception;
  4. Practice is *homo sacer*, with its reference to
  sacrifice and sacredness in opposition to constitutionalism
  (which here is represented by the university);
  5. Practice as the *bios*/state of exception is also
  an "infinite space of resistance";
  6. Practice-based research is therefore both sovereign
  in its power to supersede regulation, weak in its position
  as *homo sacer,* and an infinite place of resistance;
  7. The practitioner is thus in an unalienable, uncriticizable
  position of immanent power/abjection.

Here the distinction between art and artist is blurred.
Art (that which the artists make) and the artist's "subject
position" are often aligned in scholarship in such a way as to
maintain the incalculable space of resistance both in social,
embodied, and material terms. However, such political
subjectification brings with it a tethering—a demand for the
acknowledgement of space/time/body/matter—is to the

world of the calculable, the unjust, the binary, the sovereign-colonial. Practice-based research can't have it both ways, however: it is either free of jurisdiction or it arises from the realpolitik of contemporary life.

6

How to supervise? Eight propositions:

1. We recognize that the exceptionalism claimed by and/or on behalf of practice-based PhD research is based on the idea that practice is understood as outside of the law (the university);
2. We refute this.
3. We refuse the idea that practice's exceptionality automatically enables so-called theoretical scholarly divestment (because it is an aberration from the law/ lawless and also precarious/*homo sacer*);
4. We refute this.
5. We teach (we don't confer knowledge);
6. We don't know everything/we don't have experience of many things (we demonstrate this);
7. We are ourselves extremely partial (we argue from our own positions);
8. We become good enough.

7

Back to Moten:

Where can the work of (re)creative thinking be done in the midst of the enclosure of the art world, in the vocational enclosure of the university, in the ideological enclosure that one might call, even though both of its terms need radically to be called into question, the intellectual's public? The ascriptions of "self-taught" or "outsider" are expressions of desire and anxiety that redouble the structures of deprivation-in-privilege to which they react.[53]

In the quote I have repurposed throughout this text Moten is talking about Thornton Dial, the African American artist born to Alabama cotton plantation sharecroppers in the 1920s who worked as a metalworker for Pullman Cars, making large abstract images out of found and scrap, often industrial materials. Moten calls Dial's university the Pipe Shop, named for the studio warehouse in Bessemer Alabama Dial used as a workshop. When Moten talks about ascriptions of "self-taught" and "outsider" he is referring to the labels the art world uses to classify Dial. When Moten says that these terms are "ascriptions" that express "desire and anxiety that redouble the structures of deprivation-in-privilege to which they react" he is describing Exceptional Us. Our anxiety over exceptionalism "redoubles" our "deprivation-in-privilege." And in fact we are not exceptional; we are good enough. Moten continues: the "narrow slice of the intellectual and artistic milieu delusionally thinks of itself as central in the perennial inhabitation of a crisis."[54] Here he identifies the small-mindedness of our exceptional "deprivation-in-privilege." How to loosen the desire for deprivation-in-privilege, marked not only by replications of poverty, but also by the deprivation/privilege of exceptionalism (Agamben: *homo sacer* who *may be killed and yet not sacrificed*)?

Given the framework of supervision *per se*, with its performative role in the "vocational enclosure" machine of the university, it is hard work to maintain a political vigilance as a supervisor whose role as a conduit is regulative in the one hand and permissive on the other. But *loosening* may be a

53. Moten, 155.
54. Moten, 155.

good strategy. My response—and my practice—is to locate within any PhD project a form of domestic pleasure that, whilst enabling the exploration of strange and complex phenomena, beds these explorations in quotidian scenographies with forms of joy-in-the-doing. Importantly, this is an exercise, not a demand for a certain type of content (one may not be joyful in the content, but joyfulness is a type of method).

In using the term "good enough" I am referencing the sometimes controversial work of pediatrician and child psychotherapist D.W. Winnicott, who coined the term "good enough mother" to describe a form of parenting of babies and young children that, rather than subscribe to Kleinian theories of the "good mother" who is there for every moment of a child's emotional and physical needs, gradually and safely enables the child to learn to control their feelings of, for example, loss and separation, through a practice of removal:

> The good-enough mother starts off with an almost complete adaptation to her infant's needs, and as time proceeds she adapts less and less completely, gradually, according to the infant's growing ability to deal with her failure.[55]

If it's possible to ignore the gendered negation of this 1953 text (it is a mother; she is a failure), then I suggest that the job of the supervisor is to deflate the "perennial inhabitation of a crisis" through the quotidian exemplification of a "good enough." This by no means suggests sloppy scholarship; rather I am suggesting the tiring exceptionality of exceptionalism, when loosened, might lead to more substantive, social, pleasurable, and shareable research.

Finally, it goes without saying that we must reconfigure the university as a place of non-exceptionality. This would

55. D. W. Winnicott, "Transitional Objects and Transitional Phenomena—A Study of the First Not-Me Possession," *International Journal of Psychoanalysis* 34, no. 2 (1953): 89–97.

seem to me to be the place we need to start, that is,
if we are to accept certain conditions of state legislation,
or choose to work to change them from within; to be
reformist (this is certainly a "good enough" position).
How might a university reconfigure reward based on the
non-exception? By privileging collective work, by spreading
the modes of supervision across many skills (technical,
administrative, without professorial or scholarly jurisdiction).
In the reconfiguration of a university able to de-exeptionalize
practitioners of the art world an act of de-privileging must
take place, where no one can say; I refuse to explain/
articulate/share/open. The good-enough researcher and
their good-enough supervisors will work together with their
limitations and lack of omnipotence, without romanticizing
self-sacrifice in the face of desire-in-otherness.

ENGAGING SOIL AND WATER
Mari Mäkiranta

I can feel the river's cool water and its current through my rubber boots. I lean over, plunge my hands into the water and bring up the sample bottle. Against the light the water has a yellowish tinge to it. I see no signs of life in it. Can water die? How should we react to dead water, when bacteria and microbes are an essential aspect of the forces that sustain life and help us stay alive?

—July 14, Seurujoki River, Finland, entry in a research journal

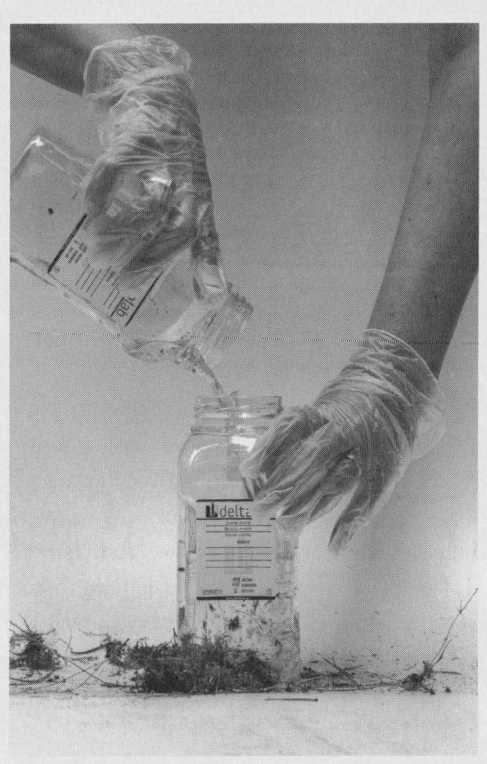

The above is an excerpt from our research journal, part of the activities of our collective Flowing Waters. The collective consists of post-doctoral artist-researchers, local people, and scientists. It is advocating for water conservation in the North and contributes opinions on the mining industry in Lapland and struggles relating to natural-resource policy. The work of the collective—nurturing the land and the water through nonviolent action, combining care and political action—has inspired this short essay. In the essay I ask what kinds of specificities, resources as stated below, are involved in supervising eco-activist and collective research and art. Since the late 2010s, artists have increasingly started to work together based on shared ideologies and aesthetics. Nevertheless, art collectives are not a new phenomenon: After the mid-1900s, collectives have been a significant part of contemporary art, to endure in times of socio-economic challenges and ecological crisis.[56]

Dismantling the modernistic conception of art has constructed a space in which conceptions of art, produced ideals, working methods, and contents have changed. The change has enabled negotiations between various conceptions and brought about new relations between art and activism. The art historical contexts of artivism (artistic activism) are rooted in German Expressionism, feminist, and avant-garde art and in the antiracist Civil Rights and antiwar movements of the 1960s. Politically transformative and activist art plays a central role in fights for social justice, such as environmental rights, gender diversity, and antiracism. Artivism not only intents to raise awareness, mobilize people, redefine traditional political or societal issues and agendas, but also to reinvent art, transform existing concepts and distinctions. Artivism seeks expressive ways of political intervention and initiates new forms of action beyond traditional paradigms of research.[57]

56. Charles Green, *The Third Hand: Collaboration in Art from Conceptualism to Postmodernism* (Minneapolis, MN: University of Minnesota Press, 2001).

57. Mari Mäkiranta and Vesa Puuronen, "Long Live Artivism," *RUUKKU—Studies in Artistic Research*, no. 20 (October 2023).

First Resource: Committing to Slow, Uncertain Changes
In Flowing Waters our activism focuses on soil and water
samples collected in areas impacted by mines, holding performances in riverine environments as well as documentation
of the performances. The soil and water samples that
the collective has gathered provide alarming evidence that the
toxic substances used in mines are inexorably making their
way through wastewaters and discharge pipes into natural
waterways in Finnish Lapland.

Artist-researchers of the collective subject themselves
in spots to what some would call irrational behavior — like
walking twenty-five kilometers on top of a discharge pipe
carrying wastewater from a mine into rivers (image 2).
Such "irrational" performances reveal power hierarchies,
draw attention to social injustices, and bring forth critical
perspectives on reality. Artivism is often associated with
shocking or provocative behavior. Flowing Waters is not out
to shock as much as it is to approach the natural environment
compassionately. The collective focuses on slow rituals in
company with the waters and the land. Characteristic of
the performances in natural surroundings are a slow settling
alongside nature, lingering in sometimes difficult riverside
terrain and gathering corporeal knowledge. What is essential
is commitment to a long-term effort and cooperation with a
range of experts, nature, communities, and other activists.
Artivism, based on the interests of a researcher, artist,
activist, or various communities, can be connected to personal
and political objectives related to subjugation, resistance, and
empowerment. Supervising eco-activist research projects
requires an understanding that activist art may also be quiet,
tentative, experimental, and searching. Sometimes, it leads
to social, environmental, institutional, and political changes.
At other times, it appears as slow, nearly invisible movements
and powers.

Activist art and research may provide the alarming evidence of environment's state in well-honed arguments, socially impactful artworks, and meticulously justified scientific findings. However, the outcomes of the research might be ignored in political decision-making processes and performances could be regarded as "irrational" and "nonconstructive." For supervision, these "failures" can reveal something with far more potential to prompt change than flawlessly realized research. In feedback sessions, "failures" can be seen as significant stages of gaining knowledge and a new perspective through "error."

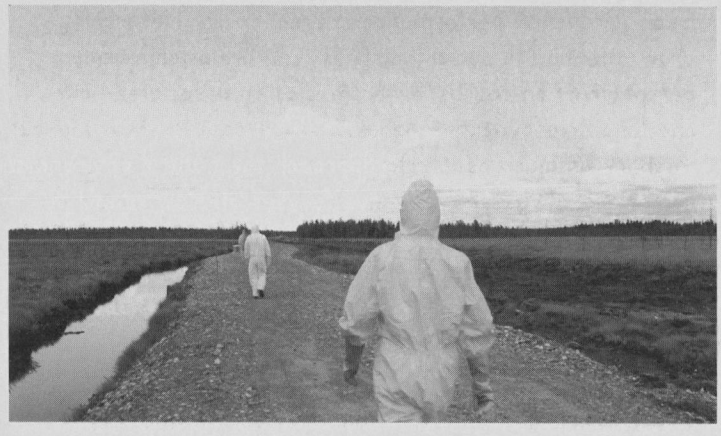

Second Resource: Rehearsing Epistemic Disobedience

The Flowing Waters collective frames its activism through historical and societal debates dealing with mining, critique of colonialism and the ideas of cultural ecofeminism.[58] Critique of colonialism and cultural ecofeminism share a

58. Boaventura de Sousa Santos, ed., *Another Knowledge Is Possible: Beyond Northern Epistemologies* (London: Verso, 2007); Boaventura de Sousa Santos, *Epistemologies of the South: Justice Against Epistemicide* (Boulder: Paradigm Publishers, 2014); Carolyn Merchant, *Radical Ecology: The Search for a Livable World* (New York: Routledge, 2005); Hanna Johansson, *Maataidetta jäljittämässä: Luonnon ja läsnäolon kirjoitusta suomalaisessa nykytaiteessa 1970–1995* (Helsinki: Like, 2005).

point of departure in epistemic disobedience. This entails critical understanding of and disengagement from the political and economic frames used to describe natural resources, narratives often featuring the resource-rich earth of the natural areas in the North. The position of the white, academically educated representatives of the mainstream population who have benefited from colonialism and residents of an area colonialized by the mining industry gives rise to a contradictory and critical epistemological horizon.

Epistemic disobedience means an effort to create connections between reality and different and unaccustomed forms of knowledge.[59] The core issue in supervising is to reflect on questions such as how the established methods used in research in the humanities and social sciences demarcate, guide, and constrict art and research praxis. Epistemic disobedience requires unlearning and contesting information produced by normative Western science, challenging the individualism embedded in the established methods of art-making and research. Artivist collaboration with the local people situated outside academia and the art world is an essential part of decolonial knowledge production and distribution.[60] As a supervisor I encourage artist-researchers to formulate concepts in collaboration with local communities, within people's ways of living. Concept creation is not only an academic practice, but it occurs in social actions, for instance in anti-mining social movements and struggles for Indigenous livelihood. The challenge for artist-researchers is to listen to, learn from, and build responsible dialogues with both human and more-than-human beings.

59. Walter D. Mignolo and Catherine E. Walsh, *On Decoloniality: Concepts, Analytics, Praxis* (Durham, NC: Duke University Press, 2018), 143.
60. Linda Tuhiwai Smith, *Decolonizing Methodologies: Research and Indigenous Peoples* (London: Zed Books, 2021).

Third Resource: Seeking New Ways to Transform the Power Structures of Art, Activism, and Research

Flowing Waters' activism is framed not only by experiences of nature but also by the theory which informs the work. In its thinking, the collective draws on colonial critique and cultural ecofeminism. Nature is not a passive object of research, waiting for engagement on the part of an artist-researcher, activist, or mine worker; it is conceived of as a nonhuman agent, as motion and force following laws of their own. In many respects, these echo the spirited "new" — materialist and post-humanist discussions in art and cultural research on the agencies of nonhuman nature, challenges to the anthropocentric mindset, and different approaches highlighting, ones that emphasize corporeality, affectivity, and materiality.[61]

Inspired by our collective's work, I encourage artist-researchers to challenge the individual ideals of authorship in research, art, and activism. I also supervise artist-researchers breaking the boundaries between different art forms and venues — moving from site-specific performance to photography and video art, from art galleries to natural environments, villages, cities, and streets. In traversing nature along rivers, the Flowing Waters collective has extended its gaze in an effort to take in the dependency between the human and nonhuman. The connectivity with other species, nature, soil, and water is something I encourage to explore deeply in eco-activist art and research. This enables seeking of the new ways of transforming the power structures of the art world and challenging the anthropocentric worldview.

61. Estelle Barrett and Barbara Bolt, *Carnal Knowledge: Towards a "New Materialism" Through the Arts* (London: I.B. Tauris, 2013); Katve-Kaisa Kontturi, *Following the Flows of Process: A New Materialist Account of Contemporary Art* (Turku, FI: Turun Yliopisto, 2012); Rick Dolphijn and Iris van der Tuin, *New Materialism: Interviews and Cartographies* (London: Open Humanities Press, 2012).

Setting and Reflecting on Conditions from Within

A prospective and retrospective toolkit for artistic and practice-based researchers and their supervisors

Download Toolkit

Developed by Iris van der Tuin (Utrecht University), Maibritt Borgen (Royal Danish Academy of Fine Arts), and Jacob Lund (Aarhus University) as part of the Novo Nordisk Foundation Visiting Professorship in Art & Art History 2021. We wish to thank the foundation as well as participants in our workshops (especially Henk Slager) and our interviewees: Guston Sondin-Kung, Lea Porsager, Maddie Leach, and Lonnie van Brummelen.

REFERENCES

Barbara Bolt, "Artistic Research — A Performative Paradigm?" in *PARSE* (2016), https://parsejournal.com/article/artistic-research-a-performative-paradigm.

Evelien Geerts and Iris van der Tuin, "Diffraction & Reading Diffractively" in *Matter* (2021), https://revistes.ub.edu/index.php/matter/article/view/33380

Rationale, or: How to Use the Toolkit

This toolkit for artistic and practice-based researchers, supervisors, and evaluators supports a multilayered approach to formulating and reflecting on the conditions of research both during the process itself and afterwards.

The toolkit invites researchers, in conversation with their peers and/or supervisors, to set the conditions of the research by working with two sets of interlinked questions and a table wherein participants note the various answers to these questions, their overlaps, and their discrepancies.

Setting the conditions from within can be done and/or repeated at various stages during a PhD-, postdoc-, or other research trajectory.

The reflective questions used can, after a project has been completed, form the starting point for evaluation and, in the case of the PhD, VALIDATION of the methods followed, formats chosen, knowledges produced, and reflections provided.

As such, the toolkit supports a prospective and retrospective reflective process that respects the performative—non-linear and unpredictable—process of artistic research.

Pick your Format(s)

Scholarly monograph
Review
Reporting article
Essay
Case study
Glossary entry
Micrology
Novel
Artwork (all genres/media, material/immaterial)
Interactive (digital) work
Immersive environment
Exhibition
Exhibition catalogue
Artist book
Zine
Poster/pamphlet
Artist talk

Lecture performance
Performative conference
Screening program
Workshop
Research lab
Walk
Activist gesture
...

Describe your Format(s Diffractively*)

EXPRESSION   What is conveyed/expressed by each or by the formats assembled?

STYLE   In what style?

ARCHIVE   What relation to an archive? What archive?

AUDIENCE   What's the audience? What publics get created?

METHOD   How to get there? How did you get there?

SITUATEDNESS   What is your situatedness in a given field?

DESIRES   What are your desires in the given field?

* Diffractions move beyond contrast and/or comparison;
the invitation is to provide words for what happens BETWEEN two or more concepts, methods, or formats.

Prospective Layer 1: Describe

Researcher, using the formats just described, fills out table for their project/practice

	EXPRESSION	STYLE	ARCHIVE	AUDIENCE	METHOD	SITUATEDNESS	DESIRES
Scholarly monograph							
Review							
Reporting article							
Essay							
Case study							
Glossary entry							
...							

Prospective Layer 2: Enrich

Researcher provides more detail by answering some analytical questions.
What urgency are you trying to impart? Why?

Answer a minimum of three questions from below list or answer all of them:

What material practice do you intend to shift with the research? In what field?*
What methodological shifts will you engage in the process?*
What may the work reveal? What may it do?*
What new concepts may emerge through the research?*
Are these new concepts meant to shift understandings and practices in the field and/or
in other discursive fields?**

Is the work to a/effect its audience aesthetically, kinaesthetically, or affectively?**
Is the work meant to shift the way we perceive the world?**

How does each of your formats support or enrich the answers to these questions?

Questions adjusted (*) or quoted directly (**) from Bolt (2016).

Title

How might your project and its (multiple) impetus(es) be condensed into a title?

A project title communicates in condensed form what your work(s) and text are meant to convey to others and, perhaps, how they are meant to convey that.

Try to formulate a title and, while you are at it, try to be brief as well as CONCEPTUAL.

NB: It is as potentially interesting to keep track of your changing project title throughout the period of your research as it is to keep a log of the answers to the questions in the toolkit. Changes can provide starting points for individual or collective reflection.

Retrospective Layer: Reflect

Supervisors and/or promotion/assessment committee answer the questions for the purpose of validation. Has an urgency been communicated and addressed convincingly?

Pick a minimum of three or all questions from below list or answer ALL of them:

How did the research shift material practice in the field?
What methodological shifts occurred through this process?
What was revealed through the work? What did it do?
What new concepts emerged through the research?
Do these new concepts shift understandings and practices in the field and/or in other discursive fields?
Does the work a/effect its audience aesthetically, kinaesthetically, or affectively?
Does the work shift the way we perceive the world?

How does each of your formats support or enrich the answers to these questions?

All questions quoted directly from Bolt (2016).

MESSAGE IN A BOTTLE:
BRIEF NOTES ON ARCHIPELAGIC THINKING AND ARTISTIC RESEARCH
Glenn Loughran

> I find it quite pleasant to pass from one atmosphere to another through crossing a border. We need to put an end to the idea of a border that defends and prevents. Borders must be permeable.[62]

In recent times archipelagos have become powerful heuristic devices to understand complexity, flow, relation, and connection in global systems.[63] Similar to the assemblage theories of Gilles Deleuze and Félix Guattari, archipelagic thinking moves beyond abstract systems-metaphors, through a complex theory of relation. Within archipelagic thinking, relation is first understood as the formation of geographic *relationships* between islands, communities, and entities. The emphasis here is on making connections that broaden our understanding of the island, beyond its representation as a radically isolated and backward place, outside of modernity. Secondly, and more poetically, *relation*, as defined by Édouard Glissant, can be understood as the dynamic interactions that take place in peripheral spaces, where identities and environments are made, unmade, and remade.[64] Expanding on these relational dynamics Michelle Stephen and Yolanda Martínez-San Miguel recently wrote, "Archipelagoes are concrete and material, spatial, geographical, and geological occurrences that have been resignified by human interaction. They involve and entail a direct reference to the

62. Manthia Diawara, "One World in Relation," *NKA Journal of Contemporary African Art 2011*, no. 28 (2011), https://doi.org/10.1215/10757163-1266639.

63. Lanny Thompson, "Heuristic Geographies: Territories and Areas, Islands and Archipelagoes," in *Archipelagic American Studies*, ed. Brian Russell Roberts and Michelle Ann Stephens, 57–73 (Durham, NC: Duke University Press, 2017).

64. Thompson, "Heuristic Geographies," 63–64.

embodied experience of space that translates into a cognitive process."[65]

To think artistic research through the lens of an archipelagic thinking is to consider how the complex assemblage of artistic research disciplines could support a relational, material, spatial, research network. From music to visual arts, circus to theater, Ireland to Sweden, Norway to Portugal, each artistic research island is an Island in a chain of islands, and each artistic research discipline is tied to an "embodied experience of space that translates into a cognitive process."[66] In this sense the first function of archipelagic thinking in artistic research could support the cultivation of relations and connections between disciplinary islands that constitute the field, its contexts, and cultures. More specifically, the second role of relation, that is the *poetics* of relation, could provide historical, theoretical, and political support for the opaque/poetic character of artistic research at a time of increasing pressure for transparency and quantification.[67]

According to philosopher Byung-Chul Han, the demand for transparency in the information society has fragmented social relations, flattened their complexity, and undermined our capacity for trust. Because trust depends on our fundamental acceptance of unknowing, of the "other," demanding total knowledge and openness amounts to an obliteration of the "other," of difference and diversity.[68] Research data that is in tune with the "transparency society," that lacks the friction and opacity of the other, is techno-scientific data. To look at this dynamic through the lens of

65. Michelle Stephens and Yolanda Martínez-San Miguel, *Contemporary Archipelagic Thinking: Toward New Comparative Methodologies and Disciplinary Formations* (London: Rowman & Littlefield Publishers, 2020), 9.

66. Stephens and Martínez-San Miguel, *Contemporary Archipelagic Thinking*, 1–2.

67. *Frascati Manual 2015: Guidelines for Collecting and Reporting Data on Research and Experimental Development*, OECD, Paris, 2015.

68. Byung-Chul Han, *The Transparency Society* (Stanford, CA: Stanford University Press, 2015), 48.

island studies is to attend to the colonial and epistemological
divisions embedded in the contemporary demand for openness
and transparency. This is the lesson learned from postcolonial
thinkers such as Édouard Glissant, who wrote "We clamor
for the right to opacity for everyone."[69]

The traditional technology for *relating* between islands
has been the ship; it is the ship that connects islands and
other islands, islands and continents, and it is within the hold
of the ship that we get the abyssal dimension of archipelagic
thinking through three distinct events, "forcing together in
the slave ship hold, the depths of the sea, and the gradual
forgetting of African origins on the Caribbean plantation."[70]
More recently, Boaventura de Sousa Santos has extended
the abyssal dimension of Glissant's thinking to argue against
the "abyssal line" that historically separates western
knowledge from everything else:

> Modern Western thinking is an abyssal thinking. It
> consists of a system of visible and invisible distinctions,
> the invisible ones being the foundation of the visible
> ones. The invisible distinctions are established through
> radical lines that divide social reality into two realms,
> the realm of "this side of the line" and the realm
> of "the other side of the line." The division is such
> that "the other side of the line" vanishes as reality,
> becomes nonexistent, and is indeed produced as
> nonexistent. Nonexistent means not existing in any
> relevant or comprehensible way of being. Whatever
> is produced as nonexistent is radically excluded
> because it lies beyond the realm of what the accepted
> conception of inclusion considers to be its other. What
> most fundamentally characterizes abyssal thinking is

69. Edouard Glissant, *Poetics of Relation*, trans. B. Wing (Ann Arbor, MI:
The University of Michigan Press, 1997), 189.
70. David Chandler and Jonathan Pugh, "Abyssal Geography," *Singapore Journal
of Tropical Geography* 44:2 (2023): 199–214, 202.

thus the impossibility of the co-presence of the two sides of the line.[71]

If archipelagic thinking proposes a relational ontology, connecting entities, islands, and disciplines, post-abyssal thinking is non-ontological, it prescribes a "groundless ground," where flux and the unfolding of knowledge take priority over its capture and calcification. Through both frameworks we can begin to navigate the complex character of opacity in artistic research processes, its productive capacity as method-in-emergence and its pressure points within the context of the Open Research Paradigm. Mapping these tensions, we can enable alternative processes of self-identification, contribution, supervision, and evaluation that are simultaneously *rooted* by disciplinary formation and *rootless* in their becoming with and through the *other*, through the *abyss*.

71. Boaventura de Sousa Santos, "Beyond Abyssal Thinking: From Global Lines to Ecologies of Knowledges," *Review—Fernand Braudel Center for the Study of Economies, Historical Systems, and Civilizations* 30, no. 1 (2007): 45-89, 45, http://www.jstor.org/stable/40241677.

WE SUPERVISE TO FIND COMRADES!
Geoff Cox

> Input is data, it has a form and a purpose. It is always
> ready to be in relation, to make a connection.
> —Denise Ferreira da Silva[72]

Cultural forms have been radically transformed by computation, but what of research itself? How do collaborative practices associated with computational and network cultures challenge the production, circulation, and supervision of research? These questions emerge from the intersection of artistic and cultural practices with computational capitalism, and the desire to find alternatives to the predominant neoliberal logistical management of knowledge production. Recognizing there is no outside as such, it remains important to challenge the relations of supervision from within, to break from its inherent individualism and managerialism, and to offer some examples of relational and connective practices that are attuned to the material systems and infrastructures through which research is instituted.

These opening comments are situated in the context of my (supervisory) work at the Centre for the Study of the Networked Image (CSNI), a research center at London South Bank University.[73] The majority of our research is undertaken through collaborative partnerships with cultural institutions, and in what follows some examples are described which have the general function of challenging institutional practices. Each in their own ways allows for a rethinking of curatorial and artistic research paradigms, and for a reassessment of the forms through which this is expressed and made public. Our working assumption is that images

72. Denise Ferreira da Silva, foreword to *All Incomplete*, by Stefano Harney and Fred Moten (Wivenhoe: Minor Compositions, 2021).
73. More on CSNI can be found at https://www.centreforthestudyof.net/.

are not singular objects, nor necessarily visual, but rather assemblages, dependent on specific software and hardware environments to be executed and rendered.[74] We think that distributed forms and collaborative practices associated with computational and network cultures can provide a useful challenge to dominant forms of supervision which perpetuate unhelpful knowledge hierarchies.

In one of our collaborative PhDs, Victoria Ivanova has worked with—and has since become research and development strategic lead for—the Arts Technologies program at Serpentine Galleries.[75] The project aims to remodel the contemporary art institution into a platform to support the development of generative, systemic, and impactful modalities for the interaction between the contemporary art field and the technology sector. The collaborative research project of Rachel Falconer sets out to do something similar, working with Whitechapel Gallery, asking how technology disrupts the value chain of contemporary art, and reflecting on the challenges and potential futures of distributed audience engagement and public programming, as well as challenging the sovereignty of the curator. By extension, we might ask how technology can disrupt the value chain of research, and thus allow for reflection on the challenges and potential futures of distributed curatorial and indeed sovereign supervisory forms.

In another case, and arguably our most developed partnership, CSNI has collaborated with The Photographers' Gallery, and in particular its digital program, on a number of PhD projects. In the first of these, Nicolas Malevé has examined how machines learn to see the world with a focus on the visual dataset ImageNet and annotation practices

74. These ideas are further developed in the collaborative text, developed in the context of the Centre for the Study of the Networked Image (CSNI) at London South Bank University. For more on this, see Geoff Cox et al., "Affordances of the Networked Image," *The Nordic Journal of Aesthetics* 30, no. 61-62 (2021), https://doi.org/10.7146/nja.v30i61-62.127857.

75. Arts Technologies programme at Serpentine Galleries, https://www.serpentinegalleries.org/arts-technologies/.

to register hidden human labor and to better understand epistemic regimes of visuality.[76] The interest in this context of supervision lies in how parallel understandings across computer science and pedagogy open up new insights for both. What can we learn about learning from the dynamics of machine learning? What might be gained from moving from a constructivist model of learning associated with Piaget (which machine learning is based on) to the radical pedagogy of Paolo Friere or bell hooks or the *undercommons* of Fred Moten and Stefano Harney? Furthermore, along similar speculative lines, what can be learned about supervision from so-called supervised and unsupervised learning?[77] It might be productive to think about some parallels here, at least to challenge lazy assumptions, even though clearly the terms mean different things in different contexts. It is noteworthy that in machine learning it is generally understood that an *unsupervised approach* to learning yields more novel and unexpected outcomes.

In a second PhD with The Photographers' Gallery, the photographic image is examined as a computational object comprised of data circulating within networks, with damaging ecological effects. Working with the title "The Image at the End of the World" (inspired by Anna Tsing's *Mushroom at the End of the World*), Marloes de Valk draws attention to the weight of image data, the hardware required to transmit, receive, and view it, how these are produced, consumed, and disposed of, to ask what alternative practices exist that try to reduce its environmental impact.[78] Taking a further reference from Tsing, the project refuses the rhetoric of

76. Nicolas Malevé, "Algorithms of Vision: Human and Machine Learning in Computa-tional Visual Culture" (PhD diss., London South Bank University 2021), https://unthinking.photography/other/algorithms-of-vision.

77. Note that in supervised learning, the algorithm "learns" from the training dataset by iteratively making predictions on the data and adjusting for the correct answer, whereas unsupervised learning processes unlabeled or raw data. See https://www.geeksforgeeks.org/supervised-unsupervised-learning/.

78. Marloes de Valk, "The Image at the End of the World," https://thephotographersgallery.org.uk/image-end-world.

progress and the dismissal of alternatives based on their scalability, and instead focuses on small-scale practices that aim at lowering the network infrastructure's environmental costs.[79] In this context it is important to reflect on the research infrastructures of the university that tend to be outsourced to big tech (such as Google, Amazon, Microsoft) that retain no interest—or indeed expertise—in education as such. These services do not facilitate safe spaces nor are focused on the free exchange and care of knowledge and learning but logistical capitalism. So, how to develop more autonomy over the technical infrastructures through which we conduct our research? In other words, how to develop alternative tools that emerge from the need to configure and maintain a more sustainable and equitable network, from sharing hosted services such as cloud and encrypted file-sharing to code distribution and version-control systems?

Clearly the tools and practices we use for our writing shape collaborative content. As an alternative to teams or Google docs, for instance, Etherpad (Pad, for short) is a customizable open-source online writing tool that flattens some of the inherent hierarchies of writing. It allows for a different model for the organization and development of projects, the making of publications, and other related research tasks that tend to follow a prescribed social relation. Authors are identifiable through colors, as usernames are optional and anonymous by default. Martino Morandi describes this as "organizational writing," quoting Michel Callon's description of "writing devices that put organization-in-action into words" and how writing in this way collectively "involves conflict and leads to intense negotiation; and such collective work is never concluded, for writing leads to endless rewriting."[80]

79. See the online publication "Damaged Earth Catalog," a reference to Stewart Brand's *Whole Earth Catalog*, at http://damaged.bleu255.com/.

80. Martino Morandi, "Constant Padology," *MARCH* (January 2023), https://march.international/constant-padology/. Morandi is quoting Michel Callon, "Writing and (Re)writing Devices as Tools for Managing Complexity," in *Complexities*, ed. John Law and Annemarie Mol (Durham, NC: Duke University Press, 2020), 203.

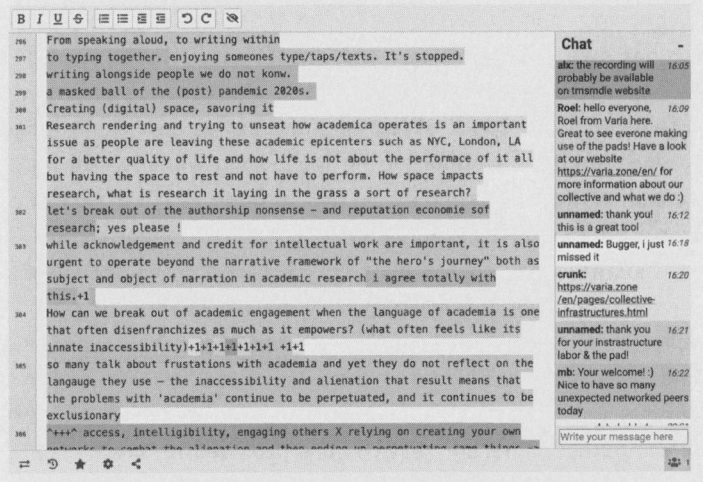

Figure 1: Screenshot of Pad from transmediale workshop (2022).

An important further principle here is that it helps to make the network infrastructure materially present, and the administration and affordance of the apparatus becomes a necessary object for critical reflection on the broader assemblage of parts.[81] In this sense, and by extension, activities such as supervision can be understood as one of care that extends beyond the prescribed relation of supervisor-supervisee to the broader sociotechnical infrastructure through which that relation is constituted. This takes its parallel in the ethics of feminist servers that question the material conditions of serving information to counter the hegemonic server-client structures of big tech.[82] To further explain and quote, a feminist server "is a situated

81. Furthermore, Etherbox, developed by Michael Murtaugh, is a local and portable version of Etherpad that runs on a small computer that creates a local wireless network without the need for an internet connection, and allows for more autonomy over the way tools and practices shape collaborative content. See *Networks of One's Own*, a playful reference to Virginia Woolf's *A Room of One's Own*, at https://networksofonesown. constantvzw.org/etherbox/manual.html, and https://networksofonesown.constantvzw.org /etherbox/manual.html#episode-1-etherbox.

82. For instance, see *A Traversal Network of Feminist Servers*, a collaborative project formed around intersectional, feminist, ecological servers, available at https://atnofs. constantvzw.org/.

technology" and "autonomous in the sense that she decides for her own dependencies," and "treats network technology as part of a social reality."[83] In this way a server can become a relatively safe space of learning and exchange of knowledge to question the formation of the technology within which the system is made operational —and through which it *serves*. ServPub is another example in which CSNI is involved, a self-hosted decentralized platform for research and practice on computational publishing, run by artists, coders, activists, collectives, scholars, researchers to build shared knowledge and resources on alternative infrastructures to serve and publish, as the name suggests.[84] Using small cheap Raspberry pi computers, different services are provided to exert more autonomy over the process of working together, and to highlight how the infrastructures of research depend on maintenance, care, trust, understanding, and collective (un)learning.

Alternatives to the server-client model can also be found in the ongoing collaboration between Digital Aesthetics Research Center at Aarhus University, CSNI, and the Berlin transmediale festival for art and digital culture.[85] Some of

83. For a fuller elaboration of feminist servers, produced as a collective outcome of a Constant meeting in Brussels, December 2013, see https://esc.mur.at/en/werk/feminist-server.

84. ServPub is the name of a working group of researchers at CSNI, Slade School of Fine Art, Aarhus University, and the grassroots community art-tech networks of In-grid, Systerserver, and Varia/CC. See https://servpub.net/.

85. The workshop and associated publications are organized by Christian Ulrik Andersen and myself, with transmediale and others. In brief, an annual open call is released based loosely on the festival theme of that year, targeting PhD students from a diverse spread of institutions as well as other artists and curators with a research practice. All accepted participants are asked to share a short essay of one thousand words and upload it to a wiki, and respond online using a linked pad, as well as in person at a three-day research workshop, at which they offer feedback and reduce their texts to five hundred words for publication in a "newspaper" that is presented and launched at the festival. Lastly, the participants are invited to submit full length articles of approximately five thousand words for the online open-access journal APRJA (see https://aprja.net/). The down/up scaling of the text is part of the pedagogy—condensing the argument to identify key arguments and then expanding it once more to substantiate claims. The final stage of the review process ensures that all articles adhere to conventional academic standards for scholarship such as double-blind review.

the tools and collective practices described thus far have been
put into action, including using online writing platforms such
as pads and other experimental publishing tools to challenge
some of the normative procedures of knowledge production,
peer review and publication. Workshop participants not only
engage with research questions and offer critical feedback
to each other, but also with the conditions for producing and
disseminating their research, as well as its institutional base,
and the infrastructures in operation. In 2023, *Toward a Minor
Tech* made this explicit, setting out to address alternatives
to major (or big) tech, and taking inspiration from Deleuze
and Guattari's essay "Kafka: Toward a Minor Literature,"[86]
and the three main characteristics identified, namely deterri-
torialization, political immediacy, and collective value. As well
as exploring our shared interests and understanding of minor
tech in terms of content, the approach was to implement
these political principles in practice.[87]

In other words, no Adobe products were used, and
all tools are freely available through the git versioning
system GitLab. Moreover, free and open-source software
development is a collective practice that challenges the
normative relations of production associated with commercial
development, such as a narrow definition of authorship and
copyright, and fixed divisions of labor, usefully extended to
the question of the reputation economy of academia and
its distribution regimes. More to the point, the publishing
platform developed for the workshop takes on a pedagogic,
if not supervisory, function allowing for an iterative approach
to thinking and learning together as part of a network of

86. Gilles Deleuze and Félix Guattari, *Kafka—Toward a Minor Literature*, trans.
Dana Polan (Minneapolis: University of Minnesota Press, [1975] 1986).
87. Subsequent newspaper and journal publications have been produced iteratively in
collaboration with Varia (an art and tech collective based in Rotterdam) using wiki-to-print
tools, based on MediaWiki software, Paged Media CSS techniques and the JavaScript
library Paged.js, which renders the PDF. See Christian Ulrik Andersen & Geoff Cox, eds.,
"Editorial: Toward a Minor Tech," *APRJA* 12, no. 1 (2023), https://doi.org/10.7146
/aprja.v12i1.140431.

connected material practices. In the latest workshop *Content/ Form*, held in 2024, the relation between content and form were even more pronounced and extended using ServPub (mentioned above); portable small computers that acted as a server and ran the wiki-to-print software to allow for more autonomy over organizational processes.[88] Both technological and social forms are brought together as part of an affective infrastructure for collective research.

In contrast to the approaches described above, it remains an oddity that academic books in the arts/humanities and social sciences are still predominantly produced as fixed objects written by individual authors and traditional publishers.[89] Experimental practices on the other hand expand upon the processual character of research and incorporate practices such as collaborative authorship, community peer review and annotation, updating, and iterative processes of developing a set of versions over time. Versioning presents "an opportunity to reflect critically on the way the research and publishing workflow is currently (teleologically and hierarchically) set up, and how it has been fully integrated within certain institutional and commercial settings."[90] An iterative approach allows for other possibilities that draw publishing and research closer together in ways that have implications for supervision beyond recording meetings on a VLE, in ways that are more open and processual, as networked objects distributed across various other spaces and temporalities. As such, and with these examples, the divisions of labor between writers, editors, designers, software developers

88. More details on the *Content/Form* workshop and tools as well as the newspaper publication can be found at https://wiki4print.servpub.net/index.php?title=Content-Form.

89. See Janneke Adema's "The Processual Book: How Can We Move Beyond the Printed Codex?" (2022), *LSE Review of Books* blog, https://blogs.lse.ac.uk /lsereviewofbooks/2022/01/21/the-processual-book-how-can-we-move-beyond-the-printed -codex/.

90. The Community-Led Open Publication Infrastructures for Monographs research project, of which Adema has been part, is an excellent resource in this respect, including the section Versioning Books from which the quote is taken. See https://compendium.copim .ac.uk/.

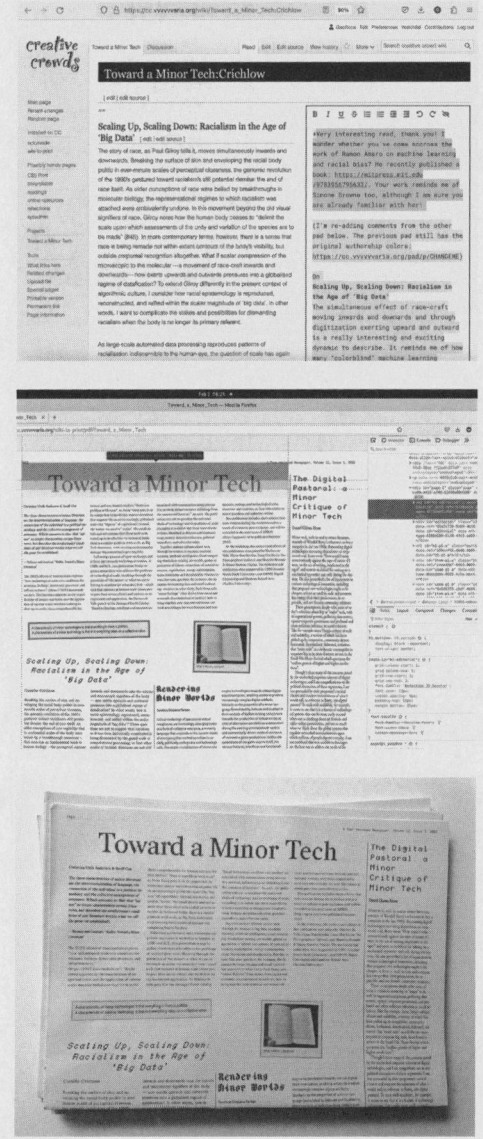

Figure 2: Screenshot of wiki and linked pad for comments.
Figure 3: Using wiki-to-print tools for layout.
Figure 4: *Toward a Minor Tech* newspaper (2023).

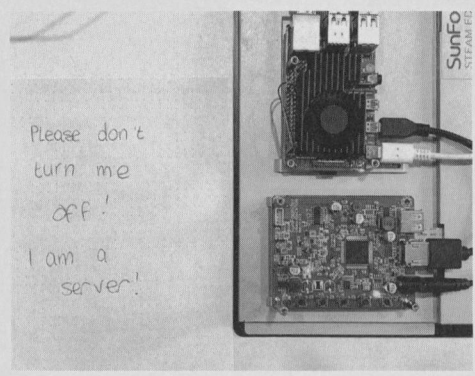

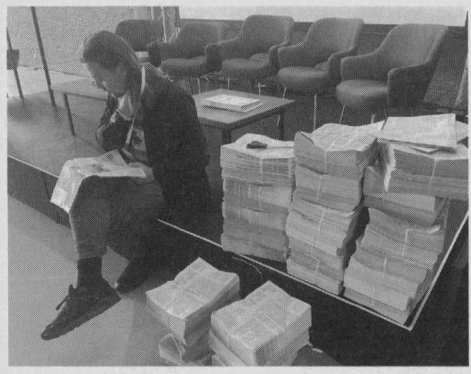

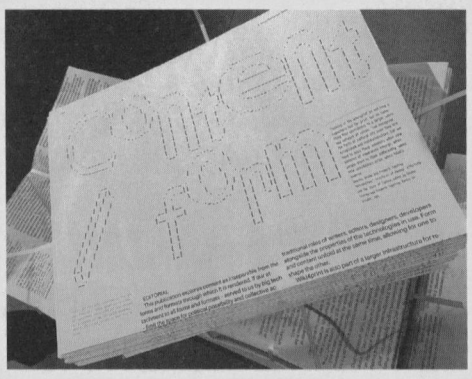

Figure 5: Raspberry pi portable server for *Content/Form* workshop, 2024.
Figure 6: *Content/Form* newspaper at transmediale festival, Berlin, February 2024.
Figure 7: *Content/Form* newspaper, launched at Haus der Kulturen der Welt, Berlin, February 2024.

are brought closer together in a nonlinear publishing workflow in which form and content unfold at the same time, allowing one to shape the other.

These principles can also be found in my collaborative book *Aesthetic Programming*, cowritten with Winnie Soon in 2021.[91] In a section on "open publishing," we emphasized that writing a book is necessarily a work in progress, "stuck in an endless loop of its own becoming."[92] If considered like software, and available in various forms including an online Git repository, encouraging new versions to be produced by others, we hoped to challenge commercial publishing conventions and illuminate our capacity to understand some of the infrastructures through which we encode our ideas and distribute them across networks. The provocation was to fork a book the way we fork software.[93] All contents are offered as an open resource, to encourage other researchers to fork a copy and customize their own versions, with different references, examples, reflections, and new chapters open for further modification and reuse. This is common practice in software development of course, particularly in the case of free and open-source software, in which developers place versions of their programs in version-control repositories (such as GitLab) so that others can download, clone, and fork them.[94]

91. Winnie Soon and Geoff Cox, *Aesthetic Programming* (London: Open Humanities Press, 2021). Link to downloadable PDF and online version can be found at https://aesthetic-programming.net/; and Git repository at https://gitlab.com/aesthetic-programming/book.

92. Soon and Cox, 21.

93. To clarify, a fork is a copy of a repository. Forking a repository allows you to freely experiment with changes without affecting the original project. Whereas versioning is the provision of a time-stamped update under the same general provisions of the original text, forking is realized by a third party that is not identical with the original author.

94. In response to the invitation to fork a copy, Mark Marino and Sarah Ciston added their chapter eight and a half (sandwiched between chapters eight and nine), Sarah Ciston and Mark C. Marino, "How to Fork a Book: The Radical Transformation of Publishing," *Medium*, 2021, https://markcmarino.medium.com/how-to-fork-a-book-the-radical-transformation-of-publishing-3e1f4a39a66c. In addition, we consider the book's translation into Chinese as a fork, on which we have been working closely with Taiwanese art and coding communities, and Taipei Arts Centre. See Shih-yu Hsu, Winnie Soon,

Put simply, the point is that by focusing on experimental publishing activities, the sharing of resources, modification of texts, and versioning, other possibilities emerge for research supervision that break out of a model of supervision constituted by tired academic procedures (and tired academics) that assume knowledge to be produced and imparted in particular ways. In terms of supervision, peer learning is an important component, in which relations are distributed more horizontally. Indeed, it's an unfortunate phrase "super-vision," the prefix I mean, as it assumes one position is above or superior to the other rather than in parallel or in reciprocal relation. It is hard not to simply associate research supervision with the managerialism that seems to pervade all current academic work. Better to turn to other possibilities suggested by affective infrastructures and to artistic research, with its potential to operate as institutional critique of established knowledge regimes and published forms, to offer more open and collaborative forms such as the examples discussed.

Importantly, the point here is not to valorize free and open-source software as if the affordances are set in advance, but to stress how technological and social forms come together, and encourage reflection on shared organizational processes and social relations. This is what Stevphen Shukaitis and Joanna Figiel argue in "Publishing to Find Comrades" (a phrase which in turn they borrow from André Breton, and which I borrow from them for this essay): "The openness of open publishing is thus not to be found with the properties of digital tools and methods, whether new or otherwise, but in how those tools are taken up and utilized within various social milieus."[95] The suggestion is not to publish preexisting knowledge and communicate this to a fixed

Tzu-Tung Lee, Chia-Lin Lee, and Geoff Cox, "Collective Translation as Forking (分岔)," *The Journal of Electronic Publishing* (forthcoming, 2024).

95. Stevphen Shukaitis and Joanna Figiel, "Publishing to Find Comrades: Constructions of Temporality and Solidarity in Autonomous Print Cultures," *Lateral* no. 8.2 (Fall 2019), https://doi.org/10.25158/L8.2.3.

reader—as is the case with much academic publishing—but to work towards developing social conditions for the coproduction of meaning, to both make something public and make publics. As they express it, "publishing is not something that occurs at the end of a process of thought, a bringing forth of artistic and intellectual labor, but rather establishes a social process where this may further develop and unfold." [96]

That one publishes to establish new social relations might be transposed to supervision, informed by what Fred Moten and Stefano Harney have described as the "logisticality of the undercommons," in contrast to the proliferation of capitalist logics exercised through the management of pedagogy and research.[97] In light of the undercommons, it would be tempting to argue for *under*-vision rather than *super*-vision here perhaps.

The further emphasis is to insist that publishing can be part of an *undervision* process—to stick with the phrase —that is collectively organized, and that can help to rupture some of the traditional hierarchies associated with academic publishing and the logistics of research practice. This is to insist that to publish, and make things public, is to generate new social relations, forged through collaboration, theft, and fugitivity (if we follow Moten and Harney). Academic publishing points to the reputation economy in which academics (and perhaps especially aspiring ones such as PhD students) provide free labor for paywalled journals—and thereby are forced to pay for articles twice over rather than steal them back—and despite the clear trend towards open access in academic publishing, relatively little has changed in practice, and scholars still seek to distribute their work through mainstream journals even when more accessible and sustainable forms are available. Similarly, these tired workflows tend to follow a model that remains relatively unchanged since

96. Shukaitis and Figiel, "Publishing to Find Comrades."
97. Stefano Harney and Fred Moten, *The Undercommons: Fugitive Planning & Black Study* (Wivenhoe: Minor Compositions, 2013).

industrialism—and arguably supervision follows the same factory logic (if we take the word supervision at face value). Attention to logistics is at the core of this, and the rejection of commercial, outsourced software and hardware and their protocols goes some way to draw attention to questions around access and control over resources and how resources shape ideas.

Finally, I refer again to Moten and Harney, who characterize the university as a site of work in which the lines between worker and management have become indistinguishable. In neoliberal institutions such as the university, the structure of supervision, which Moten and Harney understand to be a form of managerial discipline, pervades every aspect of work, and prepares students for supervision not study:

> First, students make the higher education system. Professors are primarily supervisory. Second, students working to become teachers, in any area, are—all of them—being groomed for management. Graduate students feel this contradiction and it hurts because they are moving from the shop floor to management. But the fact is that if you want to teach for money in our system, you're supposed to supervise. [...] Realizing that you have to supervise to teach for money, even lousy money, in our system can then lead to two forms of collective organization. We can take from the job our money and do something else together, or we can work to overturn a system that chains study to supervision because only this overturning is going to break that line.[98]

It is through recognition of our shared complicity in these logics, which necessarily implicates students and teachers alike, that *undercommon sociality* might develop. The need remains to challenge normative relations of supervision,

98. Harney and Moten, *All Incomplete*, 123-24.

to break away from inherent individualism and managerialism based as it is on sublimated factory logic, and open up conditions for the development of *under-vision*. We supervise to find comrades.

I DO NOT HAVE A PHD AND YET I SUPERVISE PHDS
LEE Wing Ki

Queering Identities

Subjectivity plays a vital role in the quest and thirst for knowledge in arts and humanities. It is however equally at risk to disclaim or essentialize the subjectivity of a researcher or research supervisor. Who am I? What am I? What and how does one's identities inform one's research and the research supervision? As the title suggests, I do not have a PhD and yet I supervise PhDs. Such self-statement could be controversial, as a PhD qualification may prescribe the ability to supervise PhDs. I would think otherwise; and I do otherwise. Nonetheless, the self-statement shall invite debate, criticism, and at best sharing of pedagogical practices to weave the heterogeneous nature of research supervision in contemporary arts.

Queering Methodologies

Like many of our generation in academia, we learn on the fly. The sense of becoming, the expeditious pace, and the demand to immediately engage in research supervision in academia prescribe us to supervise artistic research rather than first obtain a qualification.

Two years ago, I started the journey of co-supervising PhD projects, also being appointed to a research administration position at my institution. I have been working at the institution about a decade. Secured external research grants. Published peer-review articles. Exhibited artworks. Curated exhibitions. At the very beginning, I did not realize these attempts were instrumental to PhD supervision. Frankly, these are skillsets that a PhD researcher should have and that I can share my experience of. However, I can hardly conflate skillsets and knowledge in the realm of PhD training. One of the PhD projects examines identity formation of LGBTQIA+ and diaspora and movement of people in the context of recent Hong Kong—a meaningful project in the thick of sociopolitical turbulence and transformation in the past decades in Hong Kong and worldwide. The PhD supervisory team, in principle, is composed of me, a media artist, an eth-nographer, and a cultural theorist. The benefit of team super-vision is expansive. If I were able to provoke, I would strongly encourage cross-institution supervision and therefore intellec-tual exchange. Meanwhile we need to be mindful in handling expectation and communication between the team supervisors, and between the PhD researcher and the supervisory team.

Queering Knowledge

Artistic research has been an emerging field, even more so outside higher education in Europe and North America. Would my experience suffice to scrutinize the making of artistic research, research supervision, and the aggregated knowledge?

First and foremost, the product, in the institutional framework and regard. A typical practice-based and/or practice-led research deal is composed of the making of creative artefact(s) and a dissertation evolved from the research question, and the two are not separable and always informing and reinforcing one another. The consent of two informing components as a graduation requirement is a legacy from the UK model. Certainly, there is resistance and misconception of the components: as the terminologies inform, traditional output (that you know what it is) versus non-traditional output (that you may not know what it is); text-based and non-text-based work (and what if text is an artistic medium, a deliberate choice and a practice *per se*? Simply more to explore and question). I feel fortunate enough to be able to conduct and facilitate artistic research that may have been seen as "exceptional" and "queer" within the institution.

The British's colonial legacy in Hong Kong's higher education and other parts of the world is influential: the power of English as language and medium of instruction, for instance. The Research Assessment Exercise (and Research Excellence Framework in the future) is a prime example, as PhD supervision is one of the aspects in measuring the performance of research environment of an institution. Academic tenure, even though it was removed in the UK through the Education Reform Act, is still a pursuit amongst early career academics and PhD researchers. The neoliberalist model in higher education is ubiquitous. I am ambivalent on future development, as it will and always have been a double colonization. Yet I see the in-between space, in a city that is not essentially Eastern nor Western, to create hybrid space for pedagogical approach and new knowledge, in formats that may not be measurable and unpredictable: of unknowing, not-knowing, of urge, desire, and pleasure.

Desire and Pleasure

As much as compliance, obligation, pressure, and expectation we have been mentioning and observed, I would like to return to two operative words in governing my thinking and practice in artistic research: desire and pleasure.[99]

In the introduction to *Herculine Barbin: Being the Recently Discovered Memoirs of a Nineteenth Century French Hermaphrodite*, Michel Foucault mentions "the happy limbo of a non-identity" to describe the state of being of hermaphrodite, that best summarize my views and experiences on being queer, a queer researcher, a supervisor, and a supervisor without a PhD.[100] The quest and thirst for knowledge is a desire, also a deliberate choice. Being a

99. See Henk Slager, *The Pleasure of Research* (Ostfildern: Hatje Cantz Verlag, 2015).

100. Michel Foucault, Introduction to *Herculine Barbin: Being the Recently Discovered Memoirs of a Nineteenth-Century French Hermaphrodite*, by Herculine Barbin (Sussex: Harvester Press, [1978] 1980).

PhD supervisor is a constructed identity. The lived experience and desire supersede, if not go against, the socialization within academia and higher education. I would first advocate a nonbinary state of being a supervisor, as teaching and learning informs one another. At best, a non-identity should be cultivated and achieved. Let's undo the institutional straitjacket, exercise your power and courage to create new knowledge, navigate between spaces, create and authorize new spaces, your spaces and more spaces.

ON ACADEMIC KINSHIPS IN DOCTORAL
STUDIES IN THE ARTS
Alexandra R. Toland

"How was the relationship with your doctoral father?
Was it a relationship you'd seek to emulate?"
These were questions posed after a talk on academic
kinships I gave at the Utrecht Summer School on Supervising
Artistic and Practice-Based Research in August 2023. In
Germany, the doctoral supervisor is traditionally, informally
referred to as *Doktor-Vater* or *Doktor-Mutter* (doctoral
father or mother), indicating a hierarchical model of
kinship based on reproductive divisions of labor in biological
families that is often overtly patriarchal and reinforcing of
institutional power dynamics. The doctoral father or mother
is an "experienced master of a specific research area" with
an esteemed reputation, broad professional network, and
public standing.[101] At best, this person promotes and defends
their PhD candidates and invests time and resources in
helping them intellectually develop and successfully finish
their studies. At worst, this person can be a manipulative
or neglectful master who exploits or ignores the labor
of their doctoral students at high emotional costs. While
mentoring teams and supervisory boards are slowly replacing
the "parental" model in Germany and beyond, the concept of
kinship is still worthy of examining for purposes of community
building in doctoral education. The concept of kinship
in academia is furthermore aligned with anthropological
developments in kinship studies, which have long moved
away from references to biologically determined relationships
towards what Janet Carsten has termed "cultures of

101. "Phase #02: Distinguishing the Actors," Advancing Supervision for Artistic
Research Doctorates, 2021, accessed May 1, 2023, https://advancingsupervision.eu
/outputs/simulating-supervision-scenarios/.

relatedness."[102] As a model, academic kinship can be understood as a culture of relatedness that is based on concepts
of relational mentoring, institutional care, extra-institutional
engagement, and peer-based learning, which I will briefly
sketch out below.[103]

"It was good, but not necessarily something I seek
to emulate." After admitting to having had a mutually
supportive and overwhelmingly positive relationship with my
own doctoral father, soil physicist and arts advocate Prof.
Dr. Gerd Wessolek, for which I am still very grateful, the
discussions that occurred throughout the Utrecht Summer
School confirmed my intuitions for an expanded model of
academic kinship. The Summer School and similar events,[104]
have explored doctoral programs in the arts as particularly
fruitful places to develop alternative models of supervision.
This is in part due to their transdisciplinary nature and open-
ended, highly individualized methods for integrating practice
and theory. Most doctoral programs in the arts require
at least two mentors and encourage exchange with other
universities either by legal necessity or common interest.
The ideas presented here are thus rooted in developments
in doctoral education in the arts but can be extended to
other fields of postgraduate education. Academic kinship is
by nature relational and not exhaustive or exclusive, as it
offers the possibility of kinship not only between students and
their supervisors, but also between supervisors and other

102. Janet Carsten, *Cultures of Relatedness: New Approaches to the Study of Kinship*
(Cambridge, UK: Cambridge University Press, 2000).

103. A longer version of these considerations, based on my firsthand experience as
PhD Programme Director at the Bauhaus-Universität and secondhand knowledge of other
third cycle doctoral programmes in the arts, as presented at the summer school in Utrecht,
is available in Alexandra R. Toland, "Mother, Sister, Colleague, Friend: on Academic
Kinships in PhD Mentoring Relationships," in *Value through Design: Beiträge zu
Perspektiven Design-basierter Forschung im Kontext des Doktorats*, ed. Herbert Grüner
(St. Pölten: New Design University, 2023).

104. These include "multiplier events" hosted by the Erasmus+ Strategic Partnership
for Advancing Supervision for Artistic Research Doctorates, the ELIA working group on
Artistic Research, the Society for Artistic Research, and EARN European Artistic Research
Network.

supervisors, between supervisors and staff, and between
students and other students and a host of other individuals
inside and outside academia. From a feminist perspective,
the concept of academic kinship is also useful in thinking
about relationships as opportunities for community building
and the cultivation of institutional care. As the common adage
goes, it takes a village to raise a PhD.

In their paper, "A Relational Approach to Mentoring
Women Doctoral Students," Jo Ann Gammel and Amy
Rutstein-Riley posit relational mentoring as a process of
intellectual and emotional development for both mentor and
mentee alike. According to Gammel and Rutstein-Riley,
"the essence of relational mentoring is growth that moves
both parties to a new place whether it is greater academic
productivity, academic and professional collaborations,
or a sharing of more personal and social aspects of each
other's lives." Drawing on feminist approaches to education,
relational mentoring promotes things like "sense of worth,
clarity, productivity, desire for more connection, and
empowerment" in relationships focused on mutual care—
of research topics, of actors and participants involved, and
of the outcomes and impacts on a given community.[105] In
reference to Anne Mulvey's account of mutuality and muse-
ship in feminist research, Gammel and Rutstein-Riley go on
to describe "the nine sister goddesses" in Greek mythology.[106]
These figures appear as alternatives to the singular and
usually authoritarian mentor figure (traditionally the elder
guiding Telemachus, son of Odysseus and Penelope) who
sagely guides and oversees the journey of his protégé. In
doctoral research programs in the arts the nine sisters appear
as supportive figures with different functions who contribute

105. Jo Ann Gammel and Amy Rutstein-Riley, "A Relational Approach to Mentoring
Women Doctoral Students," New Directions for Teaching and Learning 2016, no. 147
(2016): 28, https://doi.org/10.1002/tl.20196.

106. Anne Mulvey, "Mentors, Muses, and Mutuality: Honoring Barbara Snell
Dohrenwend," Journal of Community Psychology 40, no. 1 (2012), https://doi.
org/10.1002/jcop.20507; Gammel and Rutstein-Riley, "A Relational Approach," 29.

to the journies of PhD students without much ado. These include program directors, career-center advisors, grant coordinators, university IT admins, workshop technicians, librarians, college gallery curators, engaged alumnae and postdocs, visiting professors and guest researchers, and a host of university functionaries who all contribute in various pragmatic and meaningful ways towards an individual's attainment of a doctoral degree. The contributions of the nine sisters develop for the most part dyadically and are carried out as goodwill based on shared interests or skills, or as administrative duties in what could be called instances of institutional care. Despite the responsibilities of professors stipulated in study and exam regulations, the academic kinship model recognizes and celebrates the contributions and competencies of all members of a research community. Henry Rogers and Inês Bento-Coelho have similarly highlighted the shared accountability of research institutions "in which all members of academic staff in any given faculty, division, college, or school are recognized as having a responsibility for engaging in research and for generating new knowledge."[107]

In the interest of shared responsibility, additional identities emerge beyond mothers and fathers and (at least) nine sisters: academic "aunts" acting outside direct super-visory relationships, cohorts of peers acting as "siblings" or "cousins," and alumni, emeriti, and established academics and community leaders who appear as "elders" or role models. Rogers and Bento-Coelho emphasize the importance of peer-based learning in doctoral programs in the arts, referring to David Boud and Alison Lee's definition of peer-based learning as a "reciprocal learning activity" that "involves participants

107. Henry Rogers and Inês Bento-Coelho, "Situating Supervision in the Research Environment: Re-situating Supervision in a Peer-Learning Context," *Phase #3: Improving Practices, Advanced Supervision for Artistic Research Doctorates, Erasmus+* (2021): 27, accessed May 1, 2023, https://advancingsupervision.eu/wp/wp-content/uploads/FINAL -VERSION-Situating-Supervision-in-the-Research-Environment.pdf.

learning from and with each other in both formal and
informal ways."[108] The camaraderie among PhD candidates
as "siblings" or "cousins" often characterizes the heart of
PhD programs. Structured PhD programs, compared to
individual research tracks, recognize the value of peer-
to-peer networking and support structures as something
as integral to PhD education as good supervision. Beyond
siblingship, Laura Ellingson and Patricia Sotirin propose the
practice of "academic aunting" as a "generative alternative to
mothering and sisterhood" in feminist approaches to teaching,
advising, and evaluating. The aunt is posited as a "heuristic
trope for contemporary feminist relations and political
agency" in academic contexts, a role "not bound by the
obligations of nuclear familial relationships, but [that]instead
can be entered into voluntarily or conferred on the basis of
affection and respect rather than obligation or lineage."[109]
In doctoral programs, the role of aunt is often assumed by
program directors, coordinators, and instructors, external
mentors and other figures who provide spaces
for empowerment, reflection, connectivity, and growth.
In transdisciplinary research projects, further kinship roles
emerge from extra-institutional engagement, with e.g.
representatives from local governments, community groups,
businesses, independent research institutes, museums and
cultural centers, and audience members of all ages
and kinds.

Kathleen McConnell makes a case for academic
kinship "in part because the designation of kin affords
relationships a certain weight and texture that terms such

108. David Boud, "Making the Move to Peer Learning," in *Peer Learning in Higher
Education: Learning From & With Each Other*, ed. David Boud, Ruth Cohen, and
Jane Sampson (London: Kogan Page, 2001), 9; David Boud, "Situating Academic
Development in Professional Work: Using Peer Learning," *The International Journal for
Academic Development* 4, no. 1 (1999): 6, https://doi.org/10.1080/1360144990040102.
    109. Laura L. Ellingson and Patty Sotirin, "Academic Aunting: Reimaging Feminist
(Wo)Mentoring, Teaching, and Relationships," *Women and Language* 31, no. 1 (2008):
35–36.

as coauthor, colleague, and mentor do not."[110] Despite
critique, even doctoral father/doctoral mother relationships
may fit into the kinship framing insofar as these are "based
on developing and sustaining ongoing relationships that
are mutually meaningful and involve different degrees of
reciprocity, care and emotional investment."[111] As Donna
Haraway suggests, "making kin and making kind (as in
category, care, relatives without ties by birth) stretch
the imagination and can change the story."[112] While some
relationships (e.g. supervisor/student) are largely voluntary
and others (e.g. program administrators) are not, the
story here is about the intellectual care and emotional
bonding that unfold in doctoral programs in the arts. This
bonding occurs in conventional formats of interaction as
well as spaces of designed conviviality: reading groups
and seminars, skill sharing workshops, crits, co-curated
exhibitions, co-organized symposia, conferences, informal
and formal peer reviews, as well as dinners, field trips,
and other social gatherings. According to the academic
kinship model, a PhD is shaped by all the relationships
that lead to learning and growth, cared and carried by
myriad "relatives" who contribute their time and knowledge,
emotional and intellectual support, and mutual interest in
advancing research. Looking back on discussions at the
Utrecht Summer School, I am grateful to all the other
program directors, deans, mentors and advocates of artistic
research who in their shared dedication to developing new
models of doctoral supervision and exploring spaces for
relational interaction continue to cultivate kinship across

110. Kathleen F. McConnell, "Connective Tissue, Critical Ties: Academic Collaboration
as a Form and Ethics of Kinship," *Liminalities. A Journal of Performance Studies* 8,
no. 5 (2012).

111. Hariz Halilovich, "The Ethnographer Unbared: Academic Kinship, Elective
Affinities and (Re)Negotiating Researcher Positionality," *Forum, Qualitative Social Research*
23, no. 1 (2022), https://doi.org/10.17169/fqs-23.1.3831.

112. Donna Haraway, *Staying with the Trouble: Making Kin in the Chthulucene*
(Durham, NC: Duke University Press, 2016), 103.

institutions, disciplines, languages, and national educational norms. Through this work we become a village.

SUPERVISING ART RESEARCHERS AND PERFORMATIVITY: REVERSE MENTORING, ETHICS, ADJACENCY, AND CONSILIENCE
Christa-Maria Lerm Hayes

The former Director of the UK's Secret Service (GCHQ), David Omand, recently outlined that the world has become more complex and less predictable. In order to be ready to fight the effects of climate change and general political volatility, it is important to cultivate (in my own terms) creative and lateral thinking.[113] The Dutch NATO Admiral Rob Bauer has similarly told the (Dutch) public to expect the unexpected.[114] He elaborated that, as a response, Western societies have to ready for war—not just in terms of budgetary priorities (which will of course diminish both arts and academic funding), but also in terms of attitude or "mentality." Military strategists through the ages have reiterated the truism that wars are won not on the battlefield, but in classrooms—or, by extension, universities.

Advanced (PhD level) education of art(istic) research practitioners is the topic of this volume, and I would like to approach the question of what kind of knowing and doing (performativity) art research can contribute to the urgent questions of today through the lens of the supervision of

113. In his lecture "How Spies Think: Ten Lessons in Intelligence," David Omand was summarizing the findings of his book *How to Survive a Crisis: Lessons in Resilience and Avoiding Disaster*, in Amsterdam's Zuiderkerk, December 9, 2023. He advocates taking responsibility and thinking for oneself: "people cling to the rule book when they should be prepared to tear it up if necessary." "Surviving a crisis [...] is a form of spontaneous performance art in which the cast follow an outline script [...] but then improvise the details." https://www.g10vandeeconomie.nl/speakers-en/david-omand. When I asked him why it is then that governments seem so reluctant to value (and pay for) Art(istic) Researchers and their education, i.e. support precisely those who model and apply this kind of thinking, he said that I'd be surprised how neurodiverse the intelligence community is. He thus both agreed—and pathologized art research.

114. "NAVO-admiraal: 'Samenleving moet het onverwachte gaan verwachten,'" *NOS Nieuws*, January 17, 2024, 18:47, https://nos.nl/artikel/2505275-navo-admiraal-samenleving-moet-het-onverwachte-gaan-verwachten.

researchers who investigate such projects, or through
welcoming them into academic institutions, advocating for
their work in university bureaucracies, ideally shaping
these structures to suit them, and creating cohorts of art
researchers who can be active in and beyond the academy.
Can there be—or can we perform—a sense of joint
purpose, a unity, in all the necessary, pragmatic, and
programmatic diversity that art research constitutes? And
does that contribution to our institutions, to academic work,
and to society have anything to do with the mentioned threat
of unpredictability and complexity?

I cannot begin without acknowledging "my" past PhD
researchers, many of whose projects include a practice
element to the submission.[115] They have taught (or at
least tried to teach) me both what they need and what
they can impart; and I have spent (too much?) time trying
to advocate for that in my institutions, often abandoning
(as it surely appeared) their immediate requirements in
the process (and coming close to burn-out myself). An
institutional perspective is also what I elaborated in a
chapter dealing with (creative) writing and its (belated)
entrance into artistic research debates.[116] There, my point
was that joining the field about a decade ago should not be
an occasion for celebrating certainties, but an expression
of solidarity in the margins. I then attempted to establish
art research as a "minor" field in Deleuze and Guattari's
sense (where writing is deterritorialized in relation to art,

115. At Ulster University, Belfast, National College of Art and Design, Dublin, and the
University of Amsterdam they were: Julie Louise Bacon, Áine Phillips, Marion Dowdican-
McGarry, Jeannie McCollum, Helen Sharpe, Jill Strauss, Catherine Devlin, Lyn Gallagher,
Sandra Johnston, Robert Huber, Aoife MacNamara, Emma Dwan O'Reilly, Amanda Coogan,
Andrew McClelland, Dave Loder, Martin Krenn, Megan Johnston, Maite van Dijk, Gregory
Sholette, Janice McNab, Florian Göttke, Timea Lelik, Melissa Rombout, Aga Wielocha,
Erdem Çolak, Francesca Verga, Barbara Cueto, Stacey Vorster, Matisse Huiskens.
I dedicate this chapter to them and to those who currently trust me with their supervision.

116. Christa-Maria Lerm Hayes, "Minor Literature in and of Artistic Research," in
Artistic Research and Literature, ed. Corina Caduff and Tan Wälchli (Munich: Wilhelm Fink
Verlag, 2019).

not literature).[117] In the following, I will continue developing such thoughts—as the criteria for the minor include political immediacy and communal enunciation—on the question of a joint purpose just posed. But I also want to deviate from this earlier work: solidarity now sounds too triumphalist and potentially essentialist, too similarly to the use of terms like "democracy" by people like Rob Bauer. Instead, Tina M. Campt's concept of *adjacency* will serve better—and consilience as a belief in (the need to pursue) the unity (not universality!) of enquiry across disciplines demands to be (re)claimed as the purview of art research.[118]

Following Barbara Bolt's important essay on the performativity of artistic research and its place in the academic field,[119] it is vital, indeed, to stress that small gestures and ritualized behaviors in our everyday lives have the better capacity to break the habit of norms and effect (societal) change; and that art is where unique situations and the unpredictable (as above), rather than repeatable experiments, are foregrounded. If, on this basis, shifting the focus to the supervision of art research projects, much space opens for newly thinking through and acting in academic bureaucracies.[120]

117. Gilles Deleuze and Félix Guattari, *Kafka—Toward a Minor Literature*, trans. Dana Polan (Minneapolis: University of Minnesota Press, 1986).

118. Tina M. Campt, *A Black Gaze: Artists Changing How We See* (Cambridge, MA: MIT Press, 2021). I will follow scholars like Sarat Maharaj in using "art research" rather than "artistic research" to refer to the field at stake, except for where I paraphrase the work of others, who choose the latter term.

119. Barbara Bolt, "Artistic Research: A Performative Paradigm?," *PARSE Journal*, no. 3 (Summer 2016), https://parsejournal.com/article/artistic-research-a-performative-paradigm/. Bolt points me—for the present chapter—towards art researchers "reverse mentoring" their (academic) institutions, engaging with the ethical and other conventions they find there, as well as are particularly well placed to aim towards a unity of inquiry: consilience. These thoughts also explain to me why, in art history, Aby Warburg, who focused on the "travelling" or repetition of small, "misfired" gestures (traces of affect) carried the "afterlife" of ghostly pasts better than "great" works of art—and why his work is so interesting to art researchers.

120. This shift is in line with my previous work on indirect efficacies in and of art that complement also at times necessary directness. This differentiation echoes the positions of Claire Bishop and Grant Kester in canonical social practice discourse, and I want to clarify that indirectness is, in line with Bolt, the preference on account of it achieving, where

One clear institutional role that art researchers and their supervisors can arguably aim to assume in the academy is what the museum sector already practices: reverse mentoring. Some museums have paid members of marginalized communities to give feedback on their exhibitions and all aspects of the visitor experience.[121] If institutions wish to know where they could improve, there are means and ways of achieving that. Especially if PhD researchers are funded (and that is a big "if" in many countries), it is (in my view) a justified hope or expectation that, in addition to being mentored (or supervised), they will engage in imparting their perspective and ways of knowing on the university.[122] They are more likely than others, who fit more seamlessly into this institutional frame to have made experiences that reveal where the university is less than the thoughtful, caring place that it wants to be (and says it is). They may also belong to communities that are not as yet adequately represented among the institution's staff. To find ways to listen and take seriously such feedback is important on a number of levels, of course, but not least because, as the truism goes, doing what one says and saying what one does (i.e. cognitive coherence) enhances (academic) credibility—and is a basic ingredient of leadership at all levels.[123] Art researchers arguably lead

possible, more sustained change. In some situations that is not possible: what Tania Bruguera calls "political timing specificity" is necessary to bear in mind. Claire Bishop, "Rise to the Occasion: The Art of Political Timing," *ARTFORUM* 57, no. 9 (May 2019).

121. Laura Raicovich, "A Unique Program Pays you to Visit Museums as a Guest Critic," *Hyperallergic* (June 27, 2019), https://hyperallergic.com/505841/laagp/.

122. This has an art history in the Artist Placement Group of John Latham and Barbara Steveni and, similarly from the early 1970s, the Free International University for Creativity and Interdisciplinary Research of Joseph Beuys and others. See: Christa-Maria Lerm Hayes, "Beuys's Legacy in Artist-Led University Projects," *Tate Papers*, no. 31 (Spring 2019), https://www.tate.org.uk/research/tate-papers/31/beuys-legacy-artist -led-university-projects.

123. What Achille Mbembe says about Europe can and should, in my view, be applied also to the university: decoloniality "invites us to an alternative reading of our modernity. It calls on Europe to responsibly live what it says are its origins, future, and promise. If, as Europe has always claimed, the goal of this promise really is the future of all of humanity, then postcolonial thought calls on Europe to constantly open and restart this future, in a singular manner, responsible for itself, for the Other, and before the Other. That having been said, Europe is no longer the center of the world." Achille Mbembe,

when they observe, as they tend to do, the ways in which
infrastructures are used, how resources are distributed,
where current habits and norms point to surviving hierarchies,
and injustices that are incommensurable with current
institutional mission statements, policies, and best intentions.
They often have an uncannily failsafe way of gauging
calcifications, as Andrea Philips calls them in this volume,
and that Jalal Toufic has termed a "shit detector."[124] They
can make institutions, including their supervisors, see — and
should, of course, be valued for it. Barbara Bolt elaborates:

> If, as I have argued, the aim of a performative paradigm
> is not to find correspondences but rather to recognise
> and "map" the ruptures and movements that are
> created by artistic research, then isn't that the same
> as for science? Here the work of art is not just the
> artwork/performance or event and science is not just
> the reduction of the world to data as immutable mobile.
> It *is* the effect of the work in the material, affective
> and discursive domains.[125]

One domain, where this can be the case, is the university
itself in all its breadth. To its unity, consilience, I will turn
later. Let us for the moment, though, turn to a prime location
or target of reverse mentoring: ethics.

Ethics procedures are key to how universities mind their
coherence between aspirations for excellence and what happens in individual research projects. The reverse mentoring
impetus can thus particularly include a two-way assessment of
who or what is served, e.g. when insistence on good practice
becomes gatekeeping. Assumptions that the institution is the

Out of the Dark Night: Essays on Decolonization (New York: Columbia University Press, 2021), 76.

124. Jalal Toufic, "Jalal Toufic's Notification / Notice de Jalal Toufic," ALBA website https://alba.edu.lb/english/school-of-visual-arts-Directors-Statement.

125. Bolt, "Artistic Research."

rightful arbiter in all cases cannot be left unquestioned. In many institutions, ethics reviewers are open for conversations and do appreciate the fact that the university (like the museum) has been shaped in the likeness of colonial modernity. They may even undertake steps to mitigate this. The Johannesburg Principles for Migration Research spell out actions for research design to begin to address inequality and precarity.[126]

In many cases, institutions, however, have a tendency to apply norms and "manage" diversity with metrics, which is surprising, as one of the basic tenets of academic work is to focus on what is said (the most persuasive argument), not on the identity (or position) of a human being, i.e. the academic. Adjacency, as introduced earlier, is one way of pushing against identity politics and finding modes of being with others and not to be silent in the face of their plight. This again is part of that art research process of learning to see, as well as showing and imparting that seeing in the face of what Ann Laura Stoler has called colonial aphasia.[127] The humility and often "as if" indirectness of the showing and affective evidencing that art can achieve is important in light of the feeling that we may communicate too many uncomfortable truths.

It is impossible, however, to take away that discomfort. Art research is engaging in analysis, and while that most often does not take the shape of the kinds of audits to which institutions are accustomed, the assessments that emerge are all too clear: the subject (society, its organisations and especially our academic institutions themselves) is found wanting in terms of that cognitive coherence. This is what even the most humbly presented artistic gesture communicates when it teaches (institutional) recipients to "see." (It was already Adorno's insight that all art shows how the world could be

126. The Johannesburg Principles Building Equitable and Effective Partnerships for Migration Research, https://www.migration.org.za/wp-content/uploads/2021/02/JHB-principles.pdf.

127. Ann Laura Stoler, "Colonial Aphasia: Race and Disabled Histories in France," *Public Culture* 23, no. 1 (2011): 121-26, https://doi.org/10.1215/08992363-2010-018.

otherwise). Bolt writes: "The problem for artistic research is often recognising and mapping the transformations that have occurred [through] tacit and intuitive processes that make pattern-making difficult."[128] Yet a pattern arguably does emerge: that societies, as currently governed, are heading into climate emergency, war, and discord, when all policy statements and institutional self-characterizations point into the opposite direction.

Scholars researching evaluations in the cultural field are advising that art itself, including art research, should be used to convey its value.[129] This takes art seriously as a mode of analysis. However, it doesn't account for ever more aggressive governmental demands that art justify itself—and especially its funding. When those governing feel criticized (as they have to be, given the status quo), they are less likely to fund their own—effective and most often impartial—interpreters or "auditors." Art is then subjected to unsuitable, numeric assessments the other way around, and of course devalued, its funding is denied. This may increasingly be out of a feeling of retribution, owing not to the failure, but to the stringency of the most often carefully and lovingly imparted feedback; the success of the reverse mentoring that those working in art and through its ecosystem have given.

What is to be done? Martin Warnke has cautioned that we tend to do with art what we do to one another: we should avoid pressing all detail into an (artificially) complete and hierarchical whole.[130] When—inevitably—working on complex, always incompletely understood issues, tentative language, multiple pathways to partial "solutions," several

128. Bolt, "Artistic Research," 141.

129. For the EU-funded project in which I am involved (see last note), Francesco Chiaravalloti developed such a position at a meeting of the consortium with the UvA's "Artistic Knowing" research group, September 21, 2023.

130. Martin Warnke, "Wissenschaft als Knechtungsakt," in *Stephan von Huene: What's wrong with Art?*, ed. Peter Weibel and Philipp Ziegler (Karlsruhe: ZKM, Hirmer, 2021), 53–63.

voices, methods, and "styles" will need to suffice. For me, such ambitious worlds are connected to the literature of James Joyce, who taught me to bear and enjoy not knowing. Such an impasse is also what prompted Ariella Aïsha Azoulay to formulate her vision of art as a site of working to unlearn in *Potential History: Unlearning Imperialism*.[131] Elsewhere I have argued (on the basis of Luke Gibbons's 2023 book *Joyce and the Irish Revolution*) that the literature of James Joyce formulated an alternative to colonial or authoritarian thinking as part of a "thought collective" (Ludwik Fleck) that formed around 1916.[132] History may have substituted the Catholic Church for the British Empire in Ireland, but Joyce and others developed strategies that I likened to current thinking: attitudes conveyed by Azoulay's *Potential History* and Campt's concept of adjacency. They feature empathetic immersion (interior monologues of marginalized characters), manipulation of (nonlinear) time, multiplicity of voices or styles, the use of sources in ways that privilege a repetition with a difference, etc. I traced the effects of formatively reading Joyce in and through the art writers / art researchers / curators (Carola Giedion-Welcker, Leo Steinberg, Sarat Maharaj, James Elkins and the present author with recourse to Aby Warburg as a contemporary of Joyce's). What emerged (as just one example of a piece of research among many in our field) was a commonly felt necessity to transcend disciplinary boundaries and those between interpreting and doing, the need to take art seriously by in effect becoming (fellow) art researchers and embracing this field's performativity as a working with others (and

131. Ariella Aïsha Azoulay, *Potential History: Unlearning Imperialism* (London: Verso, 2019). Isabelle Stengers's preference is to follow and evaluate (not judge), before leveraging the arguments to effect change (unless there is a need to "make a fuss"). She rethinks the relationship between scientists and politicians, suggesting "inventing-thematizing" scientists as politicians. Isabelle Stengers, *The Invention of Modern Science* (Minneapolis: University of Minnesota Press, 2000), 164–65.

132. Christa-Maria Lerm Hayes, "James Joyce and Art Writing: Indirect Efficacy, Potential (Art) History and Adjacency," in *Joyce and the Arts*, ed. Keith Williams and Cleo Hanaway-Oakley (Edinburgh: Edinburgh University Press, 2024).

since artists are often scapegoated, being with others, i.e. adjacency). In line with Joyce's dictum that his "war effort" in relation to WWI was to write *Ulysses*, we can today in and through art research establish and disseminate a discourse, where a (sharp) evaluation of society's current state is made with both humility and determination, but also transcended. Art can make one see and feel and act as a force of / for nonviolence, when considering the performativity of seeing the "ungrievables" (in Judith Butler's expression).[133]

And why is it the university — and art researchers based there — that has a role to play here? The artist John Latham was convinced that society, including the field of art in the twentieth century, had failed to account for relativity and developments in science — except for James Joyce, he told me.[134] The university is maybe a space where disciplinary gatekeepers sit, but also where, among many colleagues in all faculties, those can be found who wish to join art researchers in bearing complexities, engage in ArtScience collaborations, and more: together aim towards a unity of enquiry, what E. O. Wilson has called consilience.[135] His cross-faculty erudition is both rich in detail and immense in its aim. I wonder what Wilson (who died in 2021) would have made of the mounting evidence in his "home" discipline of biology, of the Gaia hypothesis supplanting neo- and social Darwinism more thoroughly than he (who already pushed against it) knew. He would have been pleased with my art research students and how they read across faculty boundaries not necessarily with ease, but with vivid interest. Co-location and symbiotic exchange among different organisms, and a nonhierarchical,

133. Judith Butler, *The Force of Nonviolence: An Ethico-Political Bind* (London: Verso, 2021).

134. John Latham, in conversation with the author London, April 2003. The reciprocal need for artists in universities and research in art is effectively outlined in Tom Holert, "Artistic Research: Anatomy of an Ascent," *Texte zur Kunst* 82 (June 2011).

135. Edward O. Wilson, *Consilience: The Unity of Knowledge* (London: Abacus, [1998] 2013). I thank James Elkins for mentioning this term in relation to the chapter from which I read in Utrecht.

self-regulating equilibrium as enabler of higher forms of life: this does seem to point towards a workable, consilient understanding in more areas of investigation. In addition to Lynn Margulis and James Lovelock, Karen Barad, Donna Haraway, and Isabelle Stengers are among the favourites of "my" art research students, who thus thoroughly think with and through science. Wilson wavers between according art (and its interpretation) a large and not so large role in consilience. If he had already been informed about the last quarter century's developments in art research, ArtScience, and social practice, I expect that he would have considered it as promising and exciting—if not a prime, expanding (and in itself diverse) site to find allies for consilient convergences. Such work in and on holistic fields of knowing and doing is there for others to further. I argue that entering consilience (whether it is called that or not) into discourses constitutes considerable part of the reverse mentoring that art research PhD candidates can (and also tend to) perform. They remind us that the university is a *uni*versity. Seeing consilient entanglements across the disciplines, a standing with those across divides created by colonial modernity—i.e. adjacency —appears as precisely the kind of approach that art researchers can muster.

This is also stringent as a matter of ethics bound up with art researchers' reverse mentoring of the university. According to Simon Critchley, "Ethics is anarchic meta-politics. It is the anarchic moment of democratic dissensus articulated around the experience of the ethical demand, the exorbitant demand at the heart of my subjectivity that defines that subjectivity by dividing it and opening it to otherness."[136] Walead Beshty makes the step from here to art and social practice discourse. In his view, social practice (art) and art research are

136. Simon Critchley, *Infinitely Demanding: Ethics of Commitment, Politics of Resistance* (London: Verso, 2012), 130.

concerned with "learning to inhabit the world in a better way" [...] a notion which encapsulates in lay terms what the discourse of ethics is chiefly designed to discern, i.e. a description of a mode of inhabiting the world [...] Thus the evaluation of the aesthetic condition of ethics (a barometer by which we ascertain the value and quality of interpersonal relations) has become one possibility, if not the only possibility, for the discussion of the aesthetics of the social field.[137]

Linking the present argument to the point at which it began, i.e. the role of art in facing the (un)predictabilities of the current moment, I am referring to E.O. Wilson, who devotes to ethics (and religion) the culminating penultimate chapter of his 1998 book *Consilience: The Unity of Knowledge*:

Because the success of an ethical code depends on how wisely it interprets the moral sentiments, those who frame it should know how the brain works, and how the mind develops. The success of ethics also depends on the accurate prediction of the consequences of particular actions as opposed to others, especially in cases of moral ambiguity. That too takes a great deal of knowledge consilient with the natural and social sciences. [...] The future of [art research lies] in addressing the fundamental questions of human existence head on, without embarrassment or fear [...] That of course is a very difficult task. [...] Competent people get on with them, because they need to be done.[138]

137. Walead Beshty, *Ethics*, Documents of Contemporary Art (London: Whitechapel Gallery, 2015), 18.
138. Wilson, *Consilience*, 267 and 301. He wrote "liberal arts," not art(istic) research and yet, I think that this is what the current formulation would have been, accounting for creative humanities developments, as well as art research at PhD level.

From all this, we can infer that the infrastructures of academia and art, particularly art research and social practice, are connected, or better entangled, sites of consilient inquiry and performativity. Cohorts of PhD researchers with their different concerns, but strong links through art research discourses, themselves holistic, can reach across divides, keep ethics and consilient social performativity in mind and—in line with an attitude of adjacency—impart (or live) that bearing differences and complexities is not just possible, but a basis for synergetic leaps to better (even if unpredictable) futures.

The art sector can do that too: e.g. documenta fifteen assembled social practice art, civil rights, and ecological initiatives, including many art researchers (some of them with science-driven initiatives in e.g. the realm of biodiversity and waste). And it was overshadowed by identity politics hysteria.[139] At the time of writing, we still have spaces to do this important work again, maybe to fail better in combatting the identity-politics-driven (self-)destruction underway: in both art and the university, which minds ethics and regularly and ritually assembles thought collectives-cum-"movement-of-movements" of art researchers at PhD level, their supervisors, and examiners. We have our work cut out for ourselves.[140] And yet, whenever there is a viva, a conference, seminar, an opening, or other academic or art ritual, there is an opportunity to practice, i.e. perform, the

139. In the context of the performativity of artistic research, guided by Butler, it is worth pointing out that Butler makes very clear that it (i.e. her work and the struggle of which it is an important part) was never distinctly about any one group: "It was always about equality and justice." Judith Butler, "Identity Politics and Culture Wars," *Holberg Prize Debate* 2021, https://holbergprize.org/en/2021-holberg-debate-identity-politics-and-culture-wars. On documenta fifteen see: "(un)Common Grounds: Reflecting on documenta fifteen" (symposium), FramerFramed, KNAW, Amsterdam, September 23, 2022, https://vimeo.com/showcase/9917537.

140. I mean "work" in Kevin Quashie's sense: "*work*, the craft or poiesis where what is being made is the self's project of inhabiting life rather than a product that confirms systems of capital. Kevin Everod Quashie, *Black Aliveness, Or a Poetics of Being* (Durham, NC: Duke University Press, 2021), 113. Work for Quashie thus "constitutes an ethic of relation," (130) both with regard to the self and others.

seeing of others that is central to the force of nonviolence. In such a way, we can let art-research-based consilience foster adjacency.

Writing this chapter has been enabled by the University of Amsterdam, where PhD supervision to completion attracts hours that are deducted from teaching, and the Horizon 2020 Marie Skodowska-Curie Actions (MSCA) Research and Innovation Staff Exchange (RISE) project SPACEX (number 872561. H2020-MSCA-RISE-2019), which responds to populist nationalisms and conflict in the EU, and consists to a large extent of art researchers and social practitioners in both universities and art institutions. This chapter is dedicated to the courage of UvA students, to the memory of one of them, Erick Fowler, and to the memory of victims of scholasticide.

AFTERWORD: INTO THE NEVER-NEVER
Barbara Bolt

I am taken by Geoff Cox's proposition that we supervise
to find comrades. It is so very true. Doctoral supervision is
a very lonely business. There are no blueprints for doing
it or living it, and neither the supervisor nor the graduate
researcher know where the project is going till it is done,
and then (if its worth its salt) it is only just beginning *to do
its work* in the world. That is the pain and the pleasure of
doctoral research. I had a comrade Steven Haley who, at
every orientation for new graduate researchers, would offer
the same analogy in his welcoming speech: If you are doing
honors, you are expected to be able to locate your practice
within the field and be aware of who else is working with
similar artistic concerns and methods. If you are doing a
masters project, you are required to locate your research
within the field, map the field of practice (context of practice)
and the theoretical and conceptual framework (context of
theory) that informs your research, and articulate your
methodology. In other words, you are required to lay out
the field and build the framework (fences) that provide the
context for your work. If, however, you are doing doctoral
work, you are required to survey the field, climb over the
fence, and walk into the wilderness. The "truth" is that
PhD is a journey into wilderness or the never-never.[141] It
is, as Maria Hlavajova has observed in her preface to this
volume, "thinking how things are, imagining them otherwise,
and embodying that imagination as if it were — and until it
is — possible." These are the stakes of doctoral research.
    No wonder we need comrades!

141. The never-never is a figure of speech used to describe the vast remote
area of the Australian Outback. It is a term found in literature (*We of the Never Never*
by Jeannie Gunn [1908]), poetry (*Where Dead Men Lie*, by Barcroft Boake [1889]),
and in film (Baz Luhrmann's *Australia* [2008]).

So where do we start?

We—and here I am referring to the assemblage of the candidate and the supervisor—need some form of guide stick to take us into the wilderness of space of the research. Research *must* begin with a question. *Must* is a very strong word. It is an imperative. Many artist and practice-based researchers may find the necessity of a question an irksome concept and rail against the demand: What is your research question? A question requires an answer, they say. That is not what art is! Surely. Well, NO, actually. The purpose of a research question is not concerned with exacting an answer. In fact it is not about an answer at all. Call it a question, a hypothesis, propositional, shape shifting, whatever you like. The function of the question is to open up a space and lend a hand in this enquiry rather than being understood as an instrument of enframing.

But the formulation of a question is the most difficult of things. Here I turn to Martin Heidegger's thinking on the question of the question. Heidegger is not concerned with establishing the validity of the instrument of knowledge which forms the basis of the discipline. He argues that the real "movement" in understanding must take place in the capacity of inquiry to put basic concepts in crisis, not to defend them:

> Whether or not the importance of the research always lies in such establishment of concepts, its true progress comes about not so much in collecting results and storing them in "handbooks" as in being forced to ask questions about the basic constitution of each area.[142]

Heidegger is concerned with the formulation of the question which may unsettle our preconceptions. For him, the effort to

142. Martin Heidegger, *Being and Time*, trans. J. Stambaugh (Albany, NY: State University of New York Press, 1996), 8.

retrieve the question requires that, first of all, we adequately work out the formulation of the question.[143] He proposes that asking the question of the being of beings, is itself a mode of being. Thus, for example, Heidegger argues that the discipline of history's fundamental concern is not primarily concept formation, nor is it concerned with developing a theory of historical knowledge. Rather, the concern of history is with "the interpretation of genuinely historical beings with regard to their historicality."[144]

If history is fundamentally concerned with the interpretation of historical beings with regards to their historicality, what then is the proper concern of the work of art or philosophy or any other "discipline" for that matter? In the epilogue to his essay, "The Origin of the Work of Art" (1935–36), Heidegger offers the observation that his reflections on art "are concerned with the riddle that art itself is."[145] He concedes that his reflections do not come near to solving the problem. However, solving the problem is never the point. For Heidegger, the task involved is actually to see the riddle. By posing the question, he hopes we can take some steps towards understanding the essence of art.

This is an enigmatic elegiac offering, particularly one that is staring down the face of the realities of the supervisor who may rightly see themselves, as Mick Wilson has noted, "as the agent of the institutional imposition of unfreedom." But if we are to take up Andrea Phillip's proposition that we engage in "the radical politics of generative learning," this is the space we have to open up. It is not enough for us to just understand the "essence" of art or artistic or practice-based research in itself for that matter. In the face of the "urgencies of our current condition" it is beholden upon us to actually "do" something.

143. Heidegger, 3.
144. Heidegger, 9.
145. Martin Heidegger, "The Origin of the Work of Art," in *Basic Writings*, ed. D. Farrell Krell (San Francisco: Harper and Row, 1977), 204.

And so I return to Heidegger's proposition about the "movement" in understanding that comes from the capacity of an inquiry to put basic concepts into crisis. Here I draw out a distinction between the artwork/design work and the work of art/design. The issue that remains for many researchers in the artistic and practice-based research is an adherence to the idea that new knowledge and innovation *is* the art/design work and that this should not have to be argued discursively. However, in artistic research, the novel form of the artwork is not sufficient *in itself* to articulate new knowledge and innovation.

If we are going to move beyond the production to the productivity of the work to a radical reimagining, we need terminology that will enable us to distinguish between what the work *is* (ontological) and what it *does* (the performativity of the work of art), and it is here that I part company with Heidegger's ontological take on what art is in itself to what I might call an onto-performative understanding. Elsewhere, I have differentiated between the artwork and the work of art as a way of distinguishing the work in itself and its performative potential, and, in the context of this afterword, it is valuable to return to this distinction.[146] While the terms are often used interchangeably, *the artwork* is not the same thing as *the work of art*. In this context, the artwork can be defined as the production in itself—the choreography, assemblage, design, novel, poem, screenplay, performance, painting, film, installation, drawing, or event that has emerged in and through practice—it is what is published or exhibited or performed. Its thingness, if you like. The work of art, on the other hand, is the work that the artwork *does*; it is the *movement* in concepts, understandings, methodologies, material practice, affect, and sensorial experience that arises in and through the vehicle of the work. The work that art

146. Barbara Bolt, "Artistic Research: A Performative Paradigm?," *PARSE Journal*, no. 3 (Summer 2016), https://parsejournal.com/article/artistic-research-a-performative -paradigm/.

does is its performative quality. This can relate to the process of making the work and the effects for the artistic researcher and for the field, and/or to the effects that the work may generate in the world.

The effects of the performative in art are multi-dimensional—they may be discursive, material consequences, and/or affective. How then do we assess these effects? Our task as researchers is to find ways to map the *movement* in concepts, understandings, methodologies, material practice, affect, and sensorial experience that arises in and through the research experience. This leads us back to the question of the question:

- How did the research shift material practice in the field?
- What methodological shifts occurred through this process?
- What was revealed through the work? What did it do?
- What new concepts emerged through the research?
- How these new concepts shift understandings and practices in the field and/or in other discursive fields?
- How does the work a/effect its audience aesthetically, kinaesthetically, or affectively?
- How the work shift the way we perceive the world?

The work must stand eloquently in its own way, and if it doesn't it fails. However, through mapping what the research does, artistic researchers are able to demonstrate not only how art can be understood as research, but also how its inventions may be recognized and hence articulated.

Maureen de Jager, borrowing from Janneke Adema, tells us that texts are performative in that they are reality-shaping. She observes that in "praxis writing" (and here I am using it in its broadest sense), what emerges in and through artistic and practice-based research constitutes writing *as passage*. While there are many ways of thinking about the idea of "passage" in this context we may understand the performative aspect of praxis writing as an "action or process of passing from one place, condition, or stage to another."

The idea of a passageway, a transitional space of reimagining-becoming-reality, is an exciting space of possibility but also a dangerous space, and this is the space that we as supervisors are required to negotiate and support. Heidegger uses the analogy of the passageway arguing that the "artist remains inconsequential as compared to the work, almost like a passageway that destroys itself in the creative process for the work to emerge."[147] The artistic researcher as passageway acts as the conduit through which art emerges. And in the creative process this passageway destroys itself. Once we have passed from one state to another it is not possible to go back. Those are the stakes in this work that we engage in. It is both personal and it is also political. What is essential is this "willingness" to openness and in that there is the danger of dissolution altogether and herein lies our ethical responsibility as carers and preservers.

It is the most difficult of tasks to keep our preconceptions at a distance. In order to stay with the truth that is happening in the work, we must restrain ourselves but also be there. We must let it be and not be cowered by institutional restraints nor be fear of what it may be becoming. This is the never-never of research and this is why this volume is so very important.

147. Heidegger, "The Origin of the Work of Art," 166.

BIBLIOGRAPHY

A Traversal Network of Feminist Servers. https://txt.lurk.org /ATNOFS/.

Adema, Janneke. *Living Books: Experiments in the Posthumanities.* Cambridge, MA: MIT Press, 2021.
———. "The Processual Book: How Can We Move Beyond the Printed Codex?" (2022), LSE Review of Books Blog. https://blogs .lse.ac.uk/lsereviewofbooks/2022/01/21/the-processual-book-how-can-we-move-beyond-the-printed-codex/.

Advancing Supervision for Artistic Research Doctorates. "Phase #02: Distinguishing the Actors." 2021. Accessed May 1, 2023, https://advancingsupervision.eu/outputs/simulating-supervision -scenarios/.

Agamben, Giorgio. *Homo Sacer: Sovereign Power and Bare Life.* Stanford, CA: Stanford University Press, 1995.
———. *State of Exception.* Chicago, IL: University of Chicago Press, 2005.

Andersen, Christian Ulrik, and Geoff Cox, eds., "Editorial: Toward a Minor Tech," *APRJA* 12, no. 1 (2023), https://doi.org/10.7146 /aprja.v12i1.140431.

APRJA. https://aprja.net.

Azoulay, Ariella Aisha. *Potential History: Unlearning Imperialism.* London: Verso, 2019.

Barrett, Estelle, and Barbara Bolt. *Carnal Knowledge: Towards a "New Materialism" through the Arts.* London: I.B. Tauris, 2013.

Beckett, Samuel. "Dante ... Bruno . Vico .. Joyce", In *Our Exagmination Round His Factification of Work in Progress.* Edited by Sylvia Beach, 1–22. London: Faber and Faber, 1929.

Bennett, Jill. *Practical Aesthetics: Events, Affects and Art after 9/11.* London: I.B. Tauris, 2012.

Beshty, Walead. *Ethics,* Documents of Contemporary Art. London: Whitechapel Gallery, 2015.

Bishop, Claire. "Rise to the Occasion: The Art of Political Timing." In *Artforum* (May 2019), 198–206.

Bletsas, Angelique. "The PhD Thesis as 'Text': A Post-Structuralist Encounter with the Limits of Discourse." *New Scholar* 1, no. 1 (2011): 8–22.

Bolt, Barbara. *Art Beyond Representation: The Performative Power of the Image.* London: I.B. Tauris, 2004.
———. "Artistic Research: A Performative Paradigm?" *PARSE Journal*, no. 3 (Summer 2016): 129–42.

Borgdorff, Henk. "The Production of Knowledge in Artistic Research." In *The Routledge Companion to Research in the Arts*, edited by Michael Biggs and Henrik Karlsson, 44–63. London: Routledge, 2010.

Boud, David. "Situating Academic Development in Professional Work: Using Peer Learning." *The International Journal for Academic Development* 4, no. 1 (1999): 3–10. https://doi.org/10.1080/1360 144990040102.
———. "Making the Move to Peer Learning." In *Peer Learning in Higher Education: Learning from & with Each Other*, edited by David Boud, Ruth Cohen, and Jane Sampson, 1-20. London: Kogan Page, 2001.

Bourdieu, Pierre. *Distinction: A Social Critique of the Judgement of Taste.* Cambridge, MA: Harvard University Press, 1979.

Butler, Judith. "Identity Politics and Culture Wars." In *Holberg Prize Debate* 2021, https://holbergprize.org/en/2021-holberg-debate -identity-politics-and-culture-wars.
———. *The Force of Nonviolence: An Ethico-Political Bind.* London: Verso, 2021.

Callon, Michel. "Writing and (Re)Writing Devices as Tools for Managing Complexity." In *Complexities*, edited by John Law and Annemarie Mol, 191-218. Durham, NC: Duke University Press, 2020.

Campt, Tina. *A Black Gaze: Artists Changing How We See.* Cambridge, MA: MIT Press, 2021.

Centre for the Study of the Networked Image (CSNI). https://www .centreforthestudyof.net/.

Certeau, Michel de. *The Practice of Everyday Life.* Berkeley, CA: University of California Press, 1984.

Ciston, Sarah, and Mark C. Marino. "How to Fork a Book: The Radical Transformation of Publishing." *Medium*, 2021. https://markcmarino.medium.com/how-to-fork-a-book-the-radical -transformation-of-publishing-3e1f4a39a66c.

Conty, Arianne Françoise. "Sovereign Power, Sovereign Justice: Carl Schmitt and Jacques Derrida on the State of Exception." *Philosophy Today* 62, no. 3 (2018): 939-58. https://doi.org/10.5840/philtoday20181024229.

Cox, Geoff, Annet Dekker, Andrew Dewdney, and Katrina Sluis. "Affordances of the Networked Image." *The Nordic Journal of Aesthetics* 30, no. 61–62 (2021): 40–45. https://doi.org/10.7146 /nja.v30i61-62.127857.

Critchley, Simon. *Infinitely Demanding: Ethics of Commitment, Politics of Resistance.* London: Verso, 2012.

"Damaged Earth Catalog." http://damaged.bleu255.com.

Deleuze, Gilles, and Félix Guattari. *Kafka—Toward a Minor Literature.* Translated by Dana Polan. Minneapolis, MN: University of Minnesota Press, [1975] 1986.
———. *What Is Philosophy?* Translated by Hugh Tomlinson and Graham Burchell. European Perspectives. New York, NY: Columbia University Press, [1991] 1994.

Derrida, Jacques. *Politics of Friendship.* London: Verso, 1997.

Diawara, Manthia. "One World in Relation." *NKA Journal of Contemporary African Art*, no. 28 (2011): 4-19. https://doi.org /10.1215/10757163-1266639.

Dolphijn, Rick, and Iris van der Tuin. *New Materialism: Interviews and Cartographies.* Ann Arbor, MI: Open Humanities Press, 2012.

Ellingson, Laura L., and Patty Sotirin. "Academic Aunting: Reimaging Feminist (Wo)Mentoring, Teaching, and Relationships." *Women and Language* 31, no. 1 (2008): 35–42.

European Commission. "Open Science." https://research-and -innovation.ec.europa.eu/strategy/strategy-2020-2024/our-digital -future/open-science__en.

esc medien kunst labor. "A Feminist Server." https://esc.mur.at/en /werk/feminist-server.

Experimental Publishing Compendium. https://compendium.copim
.ac.uk.

Ferreira da Silva, Denise. Foreword to *All Incomplete*, by Stefano
Harney and Fred Moten. Wivenhoe: Minor Compositions, 2021.

Foucault, Michel. Introduction to *Herculine Barbin: Being the Recently
Discovered Memoirs of a Nineteenth century French Hermaphrodite*.
Sussex: Harvester Press, [1978] 1980.

*Frascati Manual 2015: Guidelines for Collecting and Reporting
Data on Research and Experimental Development*. Organisation for
Economic Co-operation and Development, Paris, 2015.

Gammel, Jo Ann, and Amy Rutstein-Riley. "A Relational Approach
to Mentoring Women Doctoral Students." *New Directions for
Teaching and Learning* 2016, no. 147 (2016): 27–35. https://doi
.org/10.1002/tl.20196.

GeeksforGeeks. "Supervised and Unsupervised Learning." https://
www.geeksforgeeks.org/supervised-unsupervised-learning/.

Gibbons, Luke. *James Joyce and the Irish Revolution: The Easter
Rising as Modern Event*. Chicago, IL: Chicago University Press,
2023.

Glissant, Edouard. *Caribbean Discourse: Selected Essays*.
Charlottesville: University Press of Virginia, 1989.
——. *Poetics of Relation*. Translated by B. Wing. Ann Arbor:
The University of Michigan Press, 1997.

Green, Charles. *The Third Hand: Collaboration in Art from
Conceptualism to Postmodernism*. Minneapolis: University of
Minnesota Press, 2001.

Green, Michael Cawood, and Tony Williams. "On Reflection:
The Role, Mode and Medium of the Reflective Component in Practice
as Research." *TEXT* 22, no. 1 (2018). https://doi.org/10.52086
/001c.25106.

Grove, Jack. "Arts and Humanities Research Council Cuts Funded
PhDs by Quarter." *Times Higher Education*, September 10, 2023.
https://www.timeshighereducation.com/news/arts-and-humanities
-research-council-cuts-funded-phds-quarter.

Halilovich, Hariz. "The Ethnographer Unbared: Academic Kinship, Elective Affinities and (Re)Negotiating Researcher Positionality." *Forum, Qualitative Social Research* 23, no. 1 (2022). https://doi .org/10.17169/fqs-23.1.3831.

Han, Byung-Chul. *The Transparency Society*. Stanford, CA: Stanford University Press, 2015.

Haraway, Donna. *Staying with the Trouble: Making Kin in the Chthulucene*. Durham, NC: Duke University Press, 2016.

Harney, Stefano, and Fred Moten. *All Incomplete*. Wivenhoe: Minor Compositions, 2021.
———. *The Undercommons: Fugitive Planning & Black Study*. Wivenhoe: Minor Compositions, 2013.

Hayes, Christa-Maria Lerm. "Beuys's Legacy in Artist-Led University Projects." *Tate Papers*, no. 31 (Spring 2019). https://www.tate.org.uk/research/tate-papers/31/beuys-legacy -artist-led-university-projects.
———. "Minor Literature in and of Artistic Research." In *Artistic Research and Literature*, edited by Corina Caduff and Tan Wälchli, 49-62. Munich: Wilhelm Fink Verlag, 2019.
———. "James Joyce and Art Writing: Indirect Efficacy, Potential (Art) History and Adjacency." in *Joyce and the Arts*, edited by Keith Williams and Cleo Hanaway-Oakley. Edinburgh: Edinburgh University Press, 2024 (Forthcoming).

Heidegger, Martin. "The Origin of the Work of Art." In *Basic Writings*, edited by D. Farrell Krell. San Francisco: Harper and Row, 1977.
———. *Being and Time*. Translated by J. Stambaugh. Albany: State University of New York Press, 1996

Holert, Tom. "Artistic Research: Anatomy of an Ascent." *Texte zur Kunst* 82 (June 2011): 38–63.

Hsu, Shih-yu, Winnie Soon, Tzu-Tung Lee, Chia-Lin Lee, and Geoff Cox. "Collective Translation as Forking (分岔)." *The Journal of Electronic Publishing* (2024, forthcoming).

Johansson, Hanna. *Maataidetta Jäljittämässä: Luonnon Ja Läsnäolon Kirjoitusta Suomalaisessa Nykytaiteessa 1970–1995*. Helsinki: Like, 2005.

Kontturi, Katve-Kaisa. *Following the Flows of Process: A New Mate-rialist Account of Contemporary Art*. Turku: Turun Yliopisto, 2012.

Lavery, Carl. "Participation, Ecology, Cosmos." In *Reframing Immersive Theatre: The Politics and Pragmatics of Participatory Performance*, edited by James Frieze, 303-15. London: Palgrave Macmillan, 2016.

Lysaker, John. "Writing as Praxis." *The Journal of Speculative Philosophy* 28, no. 4 (2014): 521-36. https://doi.org/10.5325/jspecphil.28.4.0521.

Maharaj, Sarat. "Perfidious Fidelity: The Untranslatability of the Other." In *Art of the Twentieth Century: A Reader*. Edited by Jason Gaiger and Paul Wood, 297–303. Milton Keynes: The Open University, 2003.

Malevé, Nicolas. "Algorithms of Vision: Human and Machine Learning in Computational Visual Culture." PhD diss., London South Bank University 2021. https://unthinking.photography/other/algorithms-of-vision.

Mbembe, Achille. *Out of the Dark Night: Essays on Decolonization*. New York: Columbia University Press, 2021.

McConnell, Kathleen F. "Connective Tissue, Critical Ties: Academic Collaboration as a Form and Ethics of Kinship." *Liminalities: A Journal of Performance Studies* 8, no. 5 (2012).

Merchant, Carolyn. *Radical Ecology: The Search for a Livable World*. New York: Routledge, 2005.

Mignolo, Walter D., and Catherine E. Walsh. *On Decoloniality: Concepts, Analytics, Praxis*. Durham, NC: Duke University Press, 2018.

Morandi, Martino. "Constant Padology." *MARCH* (January 2023). https://march.international/constant-padology/.

Moten, Fred. *Black and Blur: Consent Not to Be a Single Being*. Durham, NC: Duke University Press, 2017.

Mulvey, Anne. "Mentors, Muses, and Mutuality: Honoring Barbara Snell Dohrenwend." *Journal of Community Psychology* 40, no. 1 (2012): 182–94. https://doi.org/10.1002/jcop.20507.

Mäkiranta, Mari, and Vesa Puuronen. "Long Live Artivism." *RUUKKU—Studies in Artistic Research*, no. 20 (October 2023). Network of Ones Own. https://networksofonesown.constantvzw .org/etherbox/manual.html and https://networksofonesown .constantvzw.org/etherbox/manual.html#episode-1-etherbox.

NOS Nieuws. "Navo-Admiraal: 'Samenleving Moet Het Onverwachte Gaan Verwachten'." January 17, 2024, 18:47. https://nos.nl /artikel/2505275-navo-admiraal-samenleving-moet-het-onverwachte -gaan-verwachten.

Omand, David. "How Spies Think: Ten Lessons in Intelligence." *G10 Van de Economie*, Zuiderkerk Amsterdam (December 9, 2023). https://www.g10vandeeconomie.nl/speakers-en/david-omand.

Phillips, Andrea. "Arts Organisations, Educational Institutions and the Collaborative Imperative." In *Institution as Praxis: New Curatorial Directions for Collaborative Research*, edited by Carolina Rito and Bill Balaskas. Berlin: Sternberg Press, 2020.

Quashie, Kevin Everod. *Black Aliveness, Or a Poetics of Being.* Durham, NC: Duke University Press, 2021.

Raicovich, Laura. "A Unique Program Pays You to Visit Museums as a Guest Critic." *Hyperallergic* (June 27, 2019). https://hyperallergic .com/505841/laagp/.

Rancière, Jacques. *The Politics of Aesthetics: The Distribution of the Sensible.* London: Continuum, 2004.

Rogers, Henry, and Inês Bento-Coelho. "Situating Supervision in the Research Environment: Re-situating Supervision in a Peer-Learning Context." Phase #3: Improving Practices, Advanced Supervision for Artistic Research Doctorates. Erasmus+. 2021. Accessed July 3, 2024, https://advancingsupervision.eu/wp/wp-content/uploads /FINAL-VERSION-Situating-Supervision-in-the-Research -Environment.pdf.

Rose, Jacqueline. *The Plague.* London: Fitzcarraldo, 2023.

Schmitt, Carl. *Political Theology: Four Chapters on the Concept of Sovereignty.* Chicago, IL: University of Chicago Press, 1985.
———. *The Concept of the Political.* Chicago, IL: University of Chicago Press, 1996.

Serpentine Galleries. "Arts Technologies." https://www .serpentinegalleries.org/arts-technologies/.

ServPub. "Welcome to ServPub." https://servpub.net.

Shukaitis, Stevphen, and Joanna Figiel. "Publishing to Find Comrades: Constructions of Temporality and Solidarity in Autonomous Print Cultures." *Lateral* no. 8.2 (Fall 2019). https://doi.org/10.25158/L8.2.3.

Silva, Denise Ferreira da. *Unpayable Debt*. London: Sternberg Press, 2022.

Slager, Henk. *The Pleasure of Research*. Ostfildern: Hatje Cantz Verlag, 2015.

Smith, Linda Tuhiwai. *Decolonizing Methodologies: Research and Indigenous Peoples*. London: Zed Books, 2021.

Soon, Winnie, and Geoff Cox. *Aesthetic Programming*. London: Open Humanities Press, 2021. https://aesthetic-programming.net.

Soskolne, Lise. "You and Your Crits." *PARSE Journal*, no. 2 (2015). https://parsejournal.com/article/you-and-your-crits/.

Sousa Santos, Boaventura de, ed. *Another Knowledge Is Possible: Beyond Northern Epistemologies*. London: Verso, 2007.
——— . "Beyond Abyssal Thinking: From Global Lines to Ecologies of Knowledges." *Fernand Braudel Center for the Study of Economies, Historical Systems, and Civilizations* 30, no. 1 (2007): 45–89. http://www.jstor.org/stable/40241677.
——— . *Epistemologies of the South: Justice Against Epistemicide*. Boulder: Paradigm Publishers, 2014.

Spinoza, Baruch. *Tractatus de Intellectus Emendatione*. Translated by Samuel Shirley. In *Spinoza: Complete Works*. Edited by Michael L. Morgan. Indianapolis, IN, and Cambridge, MA: Hackett, 2002..

Stengers, Isabelle. *The Invention of Modern Science*. Minneapolis: University of Minnesota Press, 2000.

Stephens, Michelle, and Yolanda Martínez-San Miguel. *Contemporary Archipelagic Thinking: Toward New Comparative Methodologies and Disciplinary Formations*. London: Rowman & Littlefield Publishers, 2020.

Stewart, Robyn. "Practice Vs Praxis: Constructing Models for Practitioner-Based Research." *TEXT* 5, no. 2 (2001): 1-8. https://doi.org/https://doi.org/10.52086/001c.35795.

Stoler, Ann Laura. "Colonial Aphasia: Race and Disabled Histories in France." *Public Culture* 23, no. 1 (2011): 121–56. https://doi.org/10.1215/08992363-2010-018.

The Johannesburg Principles Building Equitable and Effective Partnerships for Migration Research. https://www.migration.org.za/wp-content/uploads/2021/02/JHB-principles.pdf.

Toland, Alexandra R. "Mother, Sister, Colleague, Friend: On Academic Kinships in Phd Mentoring Relationships." In *Value through Design: Beiträge Zu Perspektiven Design-Basierter Forschung Im Kontext Des Doktorats*, edited by Herbert Grüner, 61–79. St. Pölten: New Design University, 2023.

Toufic, Jalal. "Jalal Toufic's Notification / Notice de Jalal Toufic." ALBA Website. https://alba.edu.lb/english/school-of-visual-arts-Directors-Statement.

(Un)Common Grounds: Reflecting on Documenta Fifteen, FramerFramed, KNAW, Amsterdam (September 23, 2022), https://vimeo.com/showcase/9917537.

Valk, Marloes de. "The Image at the End of the World." https://thephotographersgallery.org.uk/image-end-world.

Warnke, Martin. "Wissenschaft Als Knechtungsakt." In *Stephan Von Huene: What's Wrong with Art?*, edited by Peter Weibel and Philipp Ziegler. Karlsruhe: ZKM, Hirmer, 2021.

Wiki4print. "Content/Form." https://wiki4print.servpub.net/index.php?title=Content-Form.

Wilson, Edward O. *Consilience: The Unity of Knowledge*. London: Abacus, [1998] 2013.

Wilson, Mick. "Between Apparatus and Ethos: On Building a Research Pedagogy in the Arts." In *Artists with PhDs: On the New Doctoral Degree in Studio Art*, edited by James Elkins, 341–60. Washington: New Academia, 2014.
——— . "Take One Step Forward, Two Steps Back." In *Futures of Artistic Research*, edited by Jan Kaila, Anita Seppä, and Henk Slager, 183–91. Helsinki: Uniarts Helsinki, 2017.

Winnicott, D. W. "Transitional Objects and Transitional Phenomena —a Study of the First Not-Me Possession." *International Journal of Psychoanalysis* 34, no. 2 (1953).

Yountae, An. *The Decolonial Abyss: Mysticism and Cosmopolitics from the Ruins*. New York: Fordham University Press, 2020.

BIOGRAPHIES

Alexandra R. Toland is Junior Professor for Arts and Research
at the Bauhaus University Weimar, where she directs the PhD
program in Art and Design. She earned her MFA from the Dutch
Art Institute (DAI) and a doctorate degree in landscape planning from
the TU-Berlin as a DFG fellow in the Perspectives of Urban Ecology
Graduate Research Group.

Andrea Phillips is BALTIC Professor and Director of BxNU
Research Institute, Northumbria University & BALTIC Centre for
Contemporary Art. She lectures and writes about the economic
and social construction of public value within contemporary art,
the manipulation of forms of participation, and the potential of forms
of political, architectural, and social reorganization within artistic
and curatorial culture.

Barbara Bolt is a Professorial Fellow at The University of Melbourne.
She is a practicing artist and art theorist. She has copublished
*The Meeting of Aesthetics and Ethics in the Academy: Challenges
for Creative Practice Researchers in Higher Education* (Routledge,
2019), *Material Inventions: Applying Creative Arts Research*
(Bloomsbury, 2014) and *Practice as Research: Approaches to
Creative Arts Enquiry* (Bloomsbury, 2007).

Christa-Maria Lerm Hayes is Professor of Modern and
Contemporary Art History, University of Amsterdam. Until 2014,
she was Professor of Iconology in Belfast. Her books include:
W. G. Sebald's Artistic Legacies: Memory, Word and Image
(coeditor; Amsterdam University Press, 2023); *Brian O'Doherty/
Patrick Ireland: Word, Image and Institutional Critique* (editor, Valiz,
2018); *Post-War Germany and "Objective Chance": W. G. Sebald,
Joseph Beuys and Tacita Dean* (Steidl, 2011), and *Joyce in Art*
(Lilliput Press, 2004). She has curated internationally.

Geoff Cox is Professor of Art and Computational Culture and
Co-director of Centre for the Study of the Networked Image at
London South Bank University, also Adjunct at Aarhus University.
Further info at www.anti-thesis.net.

Glenn Loughran is an artist, lecturer, and researcher at the
TU Dublin School of Creative Arts. Since 2015 he has been the
course leader of the B.A in Visual Art on Sherkin Island and in
2020 he set up the archipelagic MA in Art and Environment in
West Cork. Recently he has also acted as Head of Artistic Research
in GradCAM and he is currently joint Research Co-ordinator in the
TU Dublin School of Creative Arts.

Henk Slager co-initiated the European Artistic Research Network (EARN), a network that investigates the impact of artistic research on current art education through symposia, expert meetings, and presentations. Departing from a similar focus on research, he has also (co-)produced various curatorial projects, a.o. Research Pavilion (Venice Biennale), 7th Shanghai Biennale, 5th Guangzhou Triennial, and 9th Bucharest Biennale. Henk Slager currently works at HKU University of the Arts Utrecht.

Iris van der Tuin is Professor of Theory of Cultural Inquiry at Utrecht University, where she is also university-wide Dean for Interdisciplinary Education. In 2021–22 Iris was Novo Nordisk Foundation guest professor in Art and Art History in between The Royal Danish Academy of Fine Arts and Aarhus University. She wrote *Critical Concepts for the Creative Humanities* (2022) with Nanna Verhoeff.

Jacob Lund is Associate Professor in the Department of Art History, Aesthetics & Culture, and Museology at Aarhus University, where he directs Centre for Research in Artistic Practice under Contemporary Conditions. His most recent book is *The Changing Constitution of the Present: Essays on the Work of Art in Times of Contemporaneity* (Sternberg, 2022).

Laura Guy is a Reader in Critical and Cultural Studies at Glasgow School of Art. She is editor of Phyllis Christopher's artist monograph *Dark Room: San Francisco Sex and Protest, 1988–2003* (Book Works, 2022) and co-editor with Glyn Davis of *Queer Print in Europe* (Bloomsbury Visual Arts, 2022).

LEE Wing Ki is an artist-researcher based in Hong Kong. His research and practice focus on contemporary photography, archival research, and are informed by queer theory and experience. He is currently an Associate Professor at the Academy of Visual Arts, and Associate Dean at the School of Creative Arts, Hong Kong Baptist University. He founded L♡VE, a curatorial platform for queer-friendly artists in Hong Kong.

Maibritt Borgen is Associate Professor of Art Theory and Head of the Laboratory for Arts Research at the Royal Danish Academy of Art, School of Visual Arts.

Mari Mäkiranta, Associate Professor, is a visual culture scholar and a photography artist with a background in feminist research, socially engaged art, and art activism. Currently, she is taking "artivist" actions considering gendered violence and large-scale destruction of the ecosystems in Arctic contexts. She is a long-term member of the board of RUUKKU — Studies in Artistic Research.

Maureen de Jager is an artist-researcher with an interest in writing-as-praxis. She obtained her Fine Art PhD through Kingston University, London, harnessing archival research, book-arts and performance-lectures to reflect on South Africa's traumatic history. De Jager is Fine Art HoD and Deputy Dean of the Humanities Faculty at Rhodes University.

Mick Wilson is Professor of Art, Director of Doctoral Studies, at HDK-Valand, University of Gothenburg, Sweden, and co-chair of the Centre for Art and Political Imaginary (2024–28).

PEN=0,1,1,0, WEIGHT=100, SLANT=0, SUPERNESS=0.5

The typeface used to set this series is called Meta-the-difference-between-the-two-Font (MTDBT2F), designed by Dexter Sinister in 2010 after MetaFont, a digital typography system originally programmed by computer scientist Donald Kunth in 1979.

Unlike more common digital outline fonts formats such as TrueType or Postscript, a MetaFont is constructed of strokes drawn with set-width pens. Instead of describing each of the individual shapes that make up a family of related characters, a MetaFont file describes only the basic pen path or *skeleton* letter. Perhaps better imagined as the ghost that comes in advance of a particular letterform, a MetaFont character is defined only by a set of equations. It is then possible to tweak various parameters such as weight, slant, and superness (more or less bold, italic, and a form of chutzpah) in order to generate endless variations on the same bare bones.

Meta-the-difference-between-the-two-Font is essentially the same as MetaFont, abiding the obvious fact that it swallows its predecessor. Although the result may look the same, it clearly can't be, because in addition to the software, the new version embeds its own backstory. In this sense, MTDBT2F is not only a tool to generate countless PostScript fonts, but *at least equally* a tool to think about and around MetaFont. Mathematician Douglas Hofstadter once noted that one of the best things MetaFont might do is inspire readers to chase after the intelligence of an alphabet, and "yield new insights into the elusive 'spirits' that flit about so tantalizingly behind those lovely shapes we call 'letters.'"

For instance, each volume in The Contemporary Condition is set in a new MTDBT2F, generated at the time of publication, which is to say *now.*

Dexter Sinister, 03/10/24, 12:58 PM

Trotskyism or Leninism

By Harpal Brar

Preface

One of the myths perpetrated by Trotskyites, with not inconsiderable help from the imperialist bourgeoisie, is that Leninism and Trotskyism are synonymous; that Trotsky was, after Lenin, the most brilliant and greatest Bolshevik (some even implying that Lenin was a great Trotskyist); that Trotsky was the true inheritor of Leninism, and a worthy successor to Lenin, but was, alas, deprived of his rightful place by the cunning manoeuvres of a third-class mediocrity and oriental despot to boot, i.e., Joseph Stalin. This anti-communist myth, repeated ad nauseam decade after decade in truly Goebbels fashion, not only in Trotskyite publications but also in classrooms by petty-bourgeois professors and teachers of history and sociology, not to mention the imperialist press and electronic media, this myth has acquired the force of a public prejudice. This prejudice is the product of deliberate distortion and falsification by Trotskyism and its bourgeois allies, of Marxism-Leninism, of deliberate inventions, deceptions, innuendoes, omissions and their tendentious interpretations of the history of the Great October Revolution and the revolutionary practice and role of the USSR, on the one hand, and the ignorance of those on whom these deceptions, distortions and downright falsifications are practised, on the other hand. Anyone who has made some study, let alone a deep study, of the subject cannot but be aware of the total falsity of this myth. It is the aim of this book to expose this myth and lay bare the truly reactionary, counter-revolutionary, essence of the petty-bourgeois ideology of Trotskyism, which is as irreconcilably hostile to Marxism-Leninism as is the bourgeoisie to the proletariat – notwithstanding its pseudo-Marxist, ultra-'left' and ultra-'revolutionary' terminology.

The task I set myself in this book is to show that Leninism and Trotskyism are mutually exclusive; that Trotskyism is irreconcilably opposed to Leninism; that those claiming to be Marxist-Leninists are duty bound, in the interests of the proletariat, to wage a ruthless and uncompromising struggle against Trotskyism; that they have to bury Trotskyism, as an ideological trend in the working-class movement. Further, I seek to demonstrate that after the death of Lenin in January 1924, as Leninism was upheld by the Bolshevik Party, now under the leadership of Stalin, Trotskyism continued its ceaseless onslaught on Leninism, with some tactical adjustments to the form of its attack. It now attacked Leninism and the Party's Leninist policy under the guise of attacking 'Stalinism' in the name of Leninism. For all that, Trotskyism continued its counter-revolutionary struggle against revolutionary Leninism, albeit without overtly and specifically naming Lenin as its target. Be it-said to the honour of the Bolshevik Party and to its leader, Stalin, Trotskyism was dealt blows equally as shattering as those delivered against it during Lenin's lifetime, causing it to suffer ignominious defeat. In particular I seek to emphasise three specific features of Trotskyism – features which bring it into irreconcilable contradiction with Leninism.

Three specific features of Trotskyism

1. 'Permanent revolution'

Trotskyism stands for the theory of 'permanent' revolution, failing to take into account the vast mass of the poor peasantry as a revolutionary force and reliable ally of the proletariat. As Lenin rightly pointed out, Trotsky's 'Permanent' revolution is tantamount to 'skipping' the peasant movement and "playing at the seizure of power." Any attempt at such a revolution as was advocated by Trotsky would have ended in certain failure, for it would have denied the Russian proletariat the support of its most dependable ally, the poor peasantry. Only this explains Leninism's unrelenting struggle against Trotskyism from 1905 onwards.

For its part Trotskyism regarded Leninism as a theory possessing "anti-revolutionary features" for no better reason that at the proper time Leninism correctly advocated and upheld the idea of the dictatorship of the proletariat and peasantry. Going far beyond this indignant opinion, Trotskyism asserts:

"The entire edifice of Leninism at the present time is built on lies and falsification and bears within itself the poisonous elements of its own decay." (Trotsky's letter to Chkeidze, 1913).

Leninism, on the other hand, asserts:

"Trotsky has never yet held a firm opinion on any important question of Marxism. He always contrives to worm his way into the cracks of any given difference of opinion, and desert one side for the other. At the present moment he is in the company of the Bundists and the liquidators. And these gentlemen do not stand on ceremony where the Party is concerned" (Lenin, *Collected Works*, Vol. 20 p. 448, 1914).

2. Distrust of Leninism in matters of organisation

Trotskyism stands for the distrust of Leninism, of Bolshevism, in matters of organisation. Whereas Bolshevism stands for the principle of a revolutionary proletarian party of a new type, a disciplined and monolithic Party, hostile to opportunist elements, Trotskyism stands for the co-existence of revolutionaries and opportunists and for the formation of groups, factions and coteries within a single Party. Anyone who is at all aware of the history of Trotsky's notorious August Bloc, in which the Martovites and Otzovists,[1] the Liquidators[2] and Trotskyites happily co-operated in their struggle against Bolshevism, cannot have failed to notice this liquidationist feature of Trotskyism. Thus, during this crucial historical period, whereas Leninism regarded the destruction of the August Bloc as a precondition for the development of the proletarian party, Trotskyism regarded the liquidationist August Bloc as the basis for building a 'real' party.

Throughout this entire period – from 1903 to 1917 – Lenin again and again denounced Trotsky for his "careerism", "Menshevism", "conciliationism" and "liquidationism." Here are a few samples chosen at random from scores of Lenin's writings in the same vein:

In a letter to Zinoviev dated 24 August 1909, Lenin writes: Trotsky behaves like a despicable careerist and factionalist of the Ryazanov-and-co type. Either equality on the editorial board, **subordination** to the central committee and no one's transfer to Paris except Trotsky's (the scoundrel, he wants to 'fix up' the **whole** rascally crew of 'Pravda' at our expense!) – or a break with this swindler and an exposure of him in the CO. He pays lipservice to the Party and behaves worse than any other of the factionalists." (*Collected Works*, Vol. 34, p. 400).

When Lenin was waging a life and death struggle to purge the Party of liquidators and otzovists, Trotsky, assuming the role of a conciliator, tried his worst to reconcile the Party with these two bourgeois trends. This caused Lenin to denounce Trotsky in these terms:

"In the very first words of his resolution Trotsky expressed the full spirit of the worst kind of conciliation, 'conciliation' in inverted commas, of a sectarian and philistine conciliation, which deals with 'given persons' and not the given line of policy, the given spirit the given ideological and political content of Party work.

"It is in this that the enormous difference lies between real partyism; which consists in purging the Party of liquidationism and otzovism, and the 'conciliation' of Trotsky and Co., which actually **renders the most faithful service to the liquidators and otzovists, and is therefore an evil that is all the more dangerous to the party the more cunningly, artfully and rhetorically it cloaks itself with professedly pro-party, professedly antifactional declamations.**" (*Notes of a Publicist, Collected Works*, Vol. 16, June 1910, p. 211 – emphasis added).

In November 1910, accusing Trotsky of following "in the wake of the Mensheviks, taking cover behind particularly; sonorous phrases, " of "putting before the German comrades **liberal views** with a Marxist coating." of being a master of "resonant but empty phrases, " of failing to understand and ignoring the "**economic content** of the Russian revolution, " and thereby depriving himself "of the possibility of understanding the historical meaning of the inner-Party struggle in Russia," Lenin goes on to state:

"The struggle between Bolshevism and Menshevism is... a struggle over the question whether to support the liberals or to overthrow the hegemony of the liberals over the peasantry. Therefore to attribute [as did Trotsky] our splits to the influence of the intelligentsia, to the immaturity of the proletariat, etc, is a childishly naive repetition of liberal fairy-tales."

Adding: "Trotsky distorts Bolshevism, because he has never been able to form any definite views on the role of the proletariat in the Russian bourgeois revolution."

Countering Trotsky's lies and falsifications in the German Social-Democratic press and accusing Trotsky of following a policy of "advertisement" of "shamelessness in belittling the Party and exalting himself before the Germans, " Lenin concludes:

"Therefore, when Trotsky tells the German comrades that he represents the 'general Party tendency" I am obliged to declare that Trotsky represents only his own faction and enjoys a certain amount of confidence **exclusively** among the otzovists and the liquidators." (*The Historical Meaning of the Inner-Party Struggle in Russia, Collected Works*, Vol. 16 pp. 374-392).

When Trotsky's Vienna Club, stepping up its activities, passed a resolution in November 1910 to organise a 'general Party fund for the purpose of preparing and convening a conference of the RSDLP", Lenin characterised this as a "direct step towards a split... a clear violation of Party legality and the start of an adventure in which Trotsky will come to grief."

Continues Lenin:

"It is an adventure in the ideological sense. Trotsky groups all the enemies of Marxism, he unites Potresov and Maximov, who detest the 'Lenin-Plekhanov' bloc, as they like to call it. **Trotsky unites all those to whom ideological decay is dear; all who are not concerned with the defence of Marxism**, all philistines who do not understand the reasons for the struggle and who do not wish to learn, think and discover the ideological roots of the divergence of views. At this time of confusion, disintegration, and wavering it is easy for Trotsky to become the 'hero of the hour' and gather all the shabby elements around himself. The more openly this attempt is made, the more spectacular will be the defeat." (Emphasis added).

Lenin ends this letter by calling, *inter alia*, for "struggle against the splitting tactics and the unprincipled adventurism of Trotsky." (*Letter to the Russian Collegium of the Central Committee of the RSDLP, Collected Works*, Vol. 17, pp. 17-22 – December 1910).

In December 1911, being sick and tired of Trotsky's dirty work as an attorney and diplomat for the liquidators and otzovists, Lenin, exposing Trotsky's factionalism, wrote:

"It is impossible to argue with Trotsky on the merits of the issue, because Trotsky holds no views whatever. We can and should argue with confirmed liquidators and otzovists, but it is no use arguing with a man whose game is to hide the errors of both these trends; in his case the thing to do is to expose him as a diplomat of the smallest calibre." (*Trotsky's Diplomacy and a Certain Party Platform, Collected Works*, Vol. 17 pp. 360362).

In July 1912, in a letter to the editor of Pravda, the daily legal Bolshevik paper printed in Petersburg from 5 May 1912, Lenin advises the editor not to reply to Trotsky's "disruptive and slanderous letters," adding:

"Trotsky's dirty campaign against *Pravda* is one mass of lies and slander... This intriguer and liquidator goes on lying right and left." (Collected Works, Vol. 35, pp. 40-41).

In *The Break-up of the 'August' Bloc* (March 1914), Lenin writes:

"Trotsky, however, has never had any 'physiognomy' at all; the only thing he does have is a habit of changing sides, of skipping from the liberals to the Marxists and back again, of mouthing scraps of catchwords and bombastic parrot phrases."

And: "Actually under the cover of high-sounding, empty and obscure phrases that confuse the non-class-conscious workers, Trotsky is defending the liquidators by passing over in silence the question of the 'underground' by asserting that there is no liberal labour policy in Russia, and the like.

"... Unity means rallying the majority of the workers in Russia about decisions which have long been known, and which condemn liquidationism...

"But the liquidators and Trotsky,... who tore up their own August bloc, who flouted all the decisions of the Party and dissociated themselves from the 'underground' as well as from the organised workers, are the worst splitters. Fortunately, the workers have already realised this, and all class-conscious workers are creating their own **real** unity **against** the liquidator disrupters of unity." (Collected Works, Vol. 20 pp. 158-161).

In his article *Disruption of unity under cover of outcries for unity*, written in June 1914, Lenin denounces Trotsky for his factionalism and liquidationism and exposes the utter falsity of the charge of splittism hurled by Trotsky and the liquidators at the Bolsheviks. Writing in his allegedly non-factional journal, Borba, Trotsky, having accused the Bolsheviks of splittism for the sole reason that they exposed and opposed liquidationism, goes on to admit that the Bolshevik "splittist tactics are winning one suicidal victory after another." This said, Trotsky adds:

"Numerous advanced workers, in a state of utter political bewilderment themselves often become active agents of a split."

Here is Lenin's retort to this accusation and 'explanation':

"Needless to say, this explanation is highly flattering, to Trotsky... and to the liquidators... Trotsky is very fond of using with the learned air of the expert pompous and high-sounding phrases to explain historical phenomena in a way that is flattering to Trotsky. Since 'numerous advanced workers' become 'active agents' of apolitical and Party line [Bolshevik Party line] which does not conform to Trotsky's line, Trotsky settles the question unhesitatingly, out of hand these advanced workers are 'in a state of utter political bewilderment', whereas he, Trotsky, is evidently 'in a state' of political firmness and clarity, and keeps to the right line!... And this very same

Trotsky, beating his breast, fulminates against factionalism parochialism, and the efforts of the intellectuals to impose their will on the workers!

"Reading things like these, one cannot help asking oneself. – is it from a lunatic asylum that such voices come?" (*Collected Works*, Vol. 20 pp. 327-347).

Continues Lenin: "The reason why Trotsky avoids facts and concrete references is because they relentlessly refute all his angry outcries and pompous phrases. It is very easy, of course, to strike an attitude and say: 'a crude and sectarian travesty.' Or to add a still more stinging and pompous catchphrase, such as 'emancipation from conservative factionalism.'

"But is this not very cheap? Is not this weapon borrowed from the arsenal of the period when Trotsky posed in all his splendour before audiences of high-school boys?" (*ibid.*)

Lenin concludes his article with a brilliant description of Trotsky's wavering and vacillation between the Party and the liquidators, calling him a "Tushino turncoat" appearing before the Party with incredibly pretentious claims, unwilling absolutely to reckon with **either** the Party decisions, which since 1908 have defined and established our attitude towards liquidationism, or with the experience of the present-day movement in Russia, which has actually brought about the **unity** of the majority on the basis of full recognition of the aforesaid decisions." (*ibid.*)

This brilliant description appears in the main body of this work and is, therefore, excluded from the preface.

About the same time – early 1914 – Trotsky, writing in issue no. 2 of his journal *Borba* falsely attributed to the "Polish Marxists" – not just Rosa Luxemburg – the position according to which the right to national self-determination "is entirely devoid of political content and should be deleted from the programme." This falsehood drew from Lenin the following observation:

"The obliging Trotsky is more dangerous than an enemy! Trotsky could produce no proof except 'private conversations' (i.e., simply gossip, on which Trotsky always subsists), classifying the 'Polish Marxists' in general as supporters of every article by Rosa Luxemburg...

"Trotsky has never yet held a firm opinion on any important question of Marxism. He always contrives to worm his way into the cracks of any given difference of opinion, and desert one side for the other. At the present moment he is in the company of the Bundists and the liquidators. And thee gentlemen do not stand on ceremony where the Party is concerned." (*The Right of Nations to Self-Determination, Collected Works*, Vol. 20 p. 447-8).

In his letter to Henriette Roland-Hoist, dated 8 March 1916, Lenin asks:
"What are our differences with Trotsky?"
To this question he gives the following answer:
"In brief – he is a **Kautskyite**, that is, he stands for unity with the Kaut-

skyites in the International and with Chkheidze's parliamentary group in Russia. We are absolutely against such unity ... " (*Collected Works*, Vol. 43, pp. 515-516).

Writing to Alexandra Kollontai on 17 February, 1917, Lenin says:

"...What a swine this Trotsky is – Left, phrases, and a bloc with the Right against the Zimmerwald Left!! He ought to be exposed (by you) if only in a brief letter to Sotsial-Demokrat!" (*Collected Works*, Vol. 35, p. 285).

Finally, in this letter of 19 Feb, 1917, to Inessa Armand, Lenin writes, *inter alia*:

"There is also a letter from Kollontai who... has returned to Norway from America. N. Iv. and Pavlov... had won Novy Mir, she says,... but ... Trotsky arrived, and this scoundrel at once ganged up with the Right wing of Novy Mir against the Left Zimmerwaldists!! That's it!! That's Trotsky for you!! Always true to himself, twists, swindles, poses as a Left, helps the Right, so long as he can... "(*Collected Works*, Vol. 35, p. 288).

In the light of the foregoing historic evidence, of the most impeccable and irrefutable kind, it can safely be asserted that Trotsky was during this long period – between 1903 and 1917 – a Menshevik and a liquidator who waged a most dirty and factional campaign against the Bolsheviks' attempts to build a revolutionary Party of the proletariat.

Although people with knowledge about the history of the Bolshevik Party know only too well that from 1903 to August 1917 Trotsky was a Menshevik and a liquidator, Trotskyites generally maintain a studied silence over this question or, worse still, they try and excuse him on this account. It is, therefore, very refreshing to discover some ardent Trotskyites who condemn Trotsky's Menshevism, centrism, conciliationism and factionalism. In this category fall the Trotskyites of the International Communist League (ICL) of the so-called Fourth International (the official Fourth International, of course, since each of the milliard Trotskyist organisations claims to be the official Fourth International and describes every other Trotskyist organisation as a fake – a hilarious phenomenon reminiscent of the *Life of Brian*). The ICL publish the theoretical journal *Spartacist*. The occasion for their frank admission and condemnation of Trotsky's Menshevism was the review, in *Spartacist* numbers 45 and 46, Winter 1990-91, English edition, by a certain ICL member, Daniel Dauget, of a biography of Leon Trotsky published in 1988 by Pierre Broué. Pierre Broué was a Professor at the Institute of Political Studies of Grenoble University who had been for 40 years a member of "the ostensibly Trotskyist Lambertist tendency in France" (ICL's description in the said review), i.e., of the Parti Communiste Internationale (PCI).

Broué praises Trotsky for being a "freelancer" – praise winch rouses the ICL to indignation and downright outrage. So as not to lose the full force of

ICL's fluent prose, the full burning anger and shame, and the thrust of their argument, and so as not to be accused of quoting them out of context, we reproduce here almost the entire section of the review that was concerned with Trotsky's factionalism and Menshevism between 1903 and 1917

Trotsky as "Freelancer"

"Broué's treatment of Trotsky's political activity between the decisive 1903 Bolshevik-Menshevik split and the October Revolution is at the core of his interpretation; because it is here that he deals with the debates within Russian Social Democracy over the nature, form and structure a revolutionary party must have if it is to take state power, as well as with the role of political and programmatic debate in forging such a party. After the 1903 split between the Bolsheviks and Mensheviks, Trotsky became a sort of freelancer in the party.

"Broué **praises** Trotsky for this, seeing in it the cause for Trotsky's leading role in the 1905 Revolution as chairman of the St Petersburg Soviet and his brilliant propagandist use of his trial following the 1905 defeat:

"'In fact, effectively fired from any factional obligations, at a good distance from the up and downs of the conflicts between the two main factions, satisfied in this respect with his unitary' position whose victory seemed to him assured in the future, Trotsky had his hands completely free to devote his attention and activity to the events that were unfolding in Russia...' – Broué, p. 97.

"To read this, one would conclude that Lenin's factional struggle against Menshevism was irrelevant – if not outright counterposed – to intervening in and leading the revolutionary struggle. Indeed, Broué views Trotsky's role as the leading 'conciliator' between the Bolsheviks and Mensheviks as exemplary.

"Earlier, as Broué notes, 'Trotsky, partisan of centralization and of the authority of the Central Committee ever since he bad been deported to Siberia, was seen in the émigré circles as Lenin's 'hatchet man',' At the 1903 Congress Trotsky began a **programmatic** struggle against Lenin on the question of the party. For example Trotsky opposed the sovereignty of the party congress: 'The Congress is a register, a controller, but not a creator' (*Report of the Siberian Delegation, 1903*) Although the programmatic implications were far from clear at the time, the 1903 split was a fundamental spilt on the party question Trotsky's federalist position on this question was also reflected in '*Report of the Siberian Delegation*' with his rejection of the Bolshevik definition of a party member that required 'personal participation in one of the Party bodies.' In practical terms Trotsky was in favour of the Menshevik definition of a party member as one who gave Personal assistance 'to the party – he wished to allow all the broad 'workers organisations' which existed alongside the party committees in many major Russian cities, to act in the name of the party **regardless** of their adherence to the statutes or decisions of party congresses.

"At the same time that Broué enthuses over Trotsky's independence, he mentions in passing that Trotsky was wrong on the party question during this entire period. But what he says pales in comparison with Trotsky's own judgement:

"'The deep differences that divided me from Bolshevism for a whole number of years and in many cases placed me in sharp and hostile opposition to Bolshevism, Were expressed most graphically in relation to the Menshevik faction. I began with the radically wrong perspective that the course of the revolution and the pressure of the proletarian masses would ultimately force both factions to follow the same road. Therefore I considered a split to be an unnecessary" disruption of the revolutionary forces. But because the active role in the split by with the Bolsheviks – since it was only by ruthless demarcation, not only ideological but organizational as well, that it was possible, in Lenin's opinion, to assure the revolutionary character of the proletarian party (and the entire subsequent history has fully confirmed the correctness of those policies) – my 'conciliationism' led me at many sharp turns in the road into hostile clashes with Bolshevism.' – Trotsky, *'Our Differences'* (Nov. 1924).

"The traditional 'center' and right wing of the Social Democracy were only too happy to use Trotsky's name and journalistic brilliance as a left cover for their own positions and **as a weapon against Lenin**. Thus Broué reports that 'Trotsky was on good terms with Kautsky and the 'center of the German Social Democracy until at least 1912... It was Kautsky during this period who, to Lenin's great anger, opened the pages of *'Die Neue Zeit'* and *'Vorwarts'* to Trotsky, Broué also details Trotsky's warm relations with the Austro-Marxists of Vienna, noting that he rapidly became 'the uncontested head of the Social Democratic colony in Vienna' from 1909 to 1912 .He passes rapidly over the fact that during the same period Rosa Luxemburg viewed Trotsky with 'systematic suspicion' and as a 'dubious individual', no doubt due to his ties to her right-wing opponents in the German Social Democracy.

"Broué's attitude toward Trotsky during these years is exemplified by his treatment of the infamous August bloc. The Vienna *'Pravda'* edited by Trotsky attempted to 'conciliate' the Bolshevik and Menshevik factions- – Broué approvingly quotes the professional anti-communist Leonard Schapiro's praise of the Vienna 'Pravda' for not being as polemical as the Bolshevik press. A 1910 agreement between the factions provided for Bolshevik financial support to the Vienna 'Pravda', with Kamenev (who was close to Lenin and was Trotsky's brother-in-law) responsible for administering the Bolshevik funds The agreement stipulated that the Mensheviks would get rid of their right wing, and the Bolsheviks of their left wing.

While the Bolsheviks respected the agreement, the Mensheviks did not, and in the subsequent polemics, Trotsky sided with the Mensheviks and got rid of Kamenev. Trotsky's articles, aimed at militants inside Russia who were unfamiliar with the details of the dispute, denounced the Bolsheviks as a 'conspiracy of the émigré clique.' Kautsky solicited and published several articles by Trotsky attacking the Bolsheviks, which provoked angry rejoinders not just from Lenin, but also from Plekhanov and Rosa Luxemburg. When the Bolshevik Prague Congress in 1912 proclaimed that it represented the party as a whole, Trotsky organised a unity' counter-conference in Vienna in August.

"In Trotsky's mind [the conference] was to have been the general unification, the reunification of the party. In fact, the Bolsheviks' rejection of it reduced the participants to a bloc against them, which they baptized the 'August bloc'. The Polish Social Democrats and Plekhanov also chose not to appear ... In fact, Trotsky's return to the factional arena proved particularly unfortunate. Independent of his intentions, and even of his precautions, the positions he took after the Prague conference and his role in forming the August bloc made him appear, despite himself, as the soul of a general coalition against the Bolsheviks and an indirect supporter of the 'liquidators'.' – Broué, pp. 139-140.

"Every qualifier in Broué's description of Trotsky's role in the August bloc is wrong or misleading. As is clear from Trotsky's denunciation of the Bolsheviks as an 'émigré clique', he was well aware that what Broué so delicately terms 'general unification', was a polemical cudgel with which to attack Lenin. Trotsky did not just 'appear' to be the soul of the anti-Bolshevik coalition, he was in fact that soul in that he was the most left-wing, most respected force outside the Bolsheviks. Trotsky's actions were not misconstrued 'despite himself,' but were an accurate reflection of the role he played vis-à-vis the Bolsheviks in the entire period from 1903 to at least 1915."

"The outbreak of WWI and the betrayal by the parties of the Second International most of whose leaders supported their own' governments in the bloody inter-imperialist war, shifted the grounds of dispute within the world socialist movement, forcing realignments and regroupments. Lenin and Trotsky both fought against the imperialist war, and both attended the gathering of antiwar socialists held in Zimmerwald Switzerland in September 1915." (pp. 33-34).

Be it noted in passing that the last sentence is either born out of dishonesty or simple ignorance – most likely the former – for everyone with the least knowledge about this matter knows that the Bolshevik slogan of working for the defeat of one's own government in the imperialist war then raging was countered by Trotsky with his chauvinist slogan demanding 'Neither victory nor defeat'. Further, we have provided, quotations above from Lenin to the effect that during this period Trotsky was a Kautskyite and fought against the Zimmerwald left headed by Lenin's Bolsheviks. But that does not concern us here. ICL continues:

"Broué argues that after Zimmerwald despite 'real disagreements' between Lenin and Trotsky, there was 'a reasonable prospect for a gradual rapprochement between the two men who in reality were divided only [sic] by the 1903 split, which had long since been outdated.' What Broué slides over is the fact that Lenin never repudiated the 1903 split – instead he generalized from it to a fully-formed **theoretical** position on the necessity for revolutionary cadres to organize a vanguard party, separate from reformist and centrist tendencies. Trotsky was ultimately won to Lenin's side on this question in 1917.

"There is something anachronistic and evocative of the worst aspects of French political traditions in Broué's repeated presentation of Trotsky as a simple star, freelancer, too busy being 'a leader of men' and giving brilliant speeches before and after the Revolution to have been a 'party man' or to have had the time to familiarize himself with [the] faction fights in the corridors'. Trotsky **was** a factionalist before 1917 – on the wrong side. But his program of conciliationism could never have built the sort of hard faction that could win leadership in the party, nor the kind of Party that could take state power." (p. 34).

Well said, Messrs the Trotskyites of the ICL! We think any comment on ibis would be superfluous!

All this does not, however, prevent the Trotskyites of the ICL from asserting, without as much as a blush, that Trotsky, after the death of Lenin, was best placed "to carry forward the authentic Bolshevik programme against Stalin's usurpers." Very strange logic indeed, according to which Trotsky, the Menshevik liquidator, who, spent two decades in a mortal struggle against every aspect of Leninism, was better suited to, carrying out the 'authentic' Bolshevik programme than someone like Stalin who, had spent two and a half decades faithfully supporting and actually carrying out the Bolshevik programme. Here is how ICL put it:

"In his admiration for Trotsky the left-Menshevik, Broué also never considers the potential authority that Trotsky would have gained and retained among stalwart Bolsheviks had he come over to Lenin's side as a hard party man in 1903 – an authority that would have served him well in the subsequent period when he fought to carry forward the authentic Bolshevik programme against Stalin's usurpers." (*Ibid.* p. 35).

Pigs might fly! The above statement of ICL amounts, if it amounts to anything at all, to a meaningless tautology, namely, had Trotsky been a staunch supporter of Leninism in the period 1903-17, he would have been well placed to carry out the authentic Bolshevik programme after Lenin's death. The problem, however, is that he was not during this long period, nor was he in the subsequent period, a staunch supporter of Leninism. The one who *was* a staunch Leninist, namely Joseph Stalin, was quite correctly chosen by the Bolshevik Party to lead it in carrying forward the authentic Bolshevik programme against the would-be usurper, to wit, Trotsky.

There is method in ICL's madness. They admit Trotsky's pre-1917 Menshevism in order to present gullible, readers with a sanitised version of Trotsky who, it is claimed, suddenly saw the light and after 1917 became a better Bolshevik than anyone else.

"The fact is," write the ICl, "that Broué... **agrees** with Trotsky's conciliationism before 1917, and much prefers Trotsky the anti-Leninist to Trotsky the Bolshevik."

Unlike Broué, in a vain attempt to gain credibility for Trotskyism, the ICL would rather make a clean admission of Trotsky's pre-1917 Menshevism and anti-Leninism in order to be able all the more zealously to fasten the label of staunch Leninist on Trotsky's lapel. This trick will not work, however, for apart from the short period during October when he hid his anti-Leninist stock-in-trade in the cupboard, Trotsky continued to practise his anti-Leninism, his anti-Bolshevism, with a zeal worthy of a better cause. It is not only the case that Broué, as is justly claimed by the ICI, "subtly puts Lenin under the gun" in order to gain the appreciation of the "anti- Leninist Soviet intelligentsia" (these words were written in the winter of 1990-91), but also the fact that the Trotskyites of the ICI, in common with all other Trotskyites, are attempting to substitute Trotskyism for Leninism, albeit by denouncing pre-1917 Trotskyism. No subterfuges, no tricks, no artful dodging, no deception, can detract from this fact – not even the pretence of praising Leninism.

3. Distrust of Bolshevik leadership

Trotsky stands for the distrust of the leaders of Bolshevism, for discrediting and defaming them. As Stalin correctly observed:

"I do not know of a single trend in the party that could compare with Trotskyism in the matter of discrediting the leaders of Leninism or the central institutions of the Party." (*Collected Works,* Vol. 6, p. 366).

In Trotsky's letter to Chkeidze, already cited, Trotsky described Lenin as "a professional exploiter of every kind of backwardness in the Russian working-class movement."

If Trotsky could express such ill-mannered views about Leninism, is there anything surprising in the fact that he showered, after Lenin's death, even more vile abuse on Lenin's most faithful pupil, Stalin.

How could Trotsky end up in Bolshevik ranks?

How was it that Trotsky, having such an impeccably anti-Bolshevik and anti-Leninist record, found himself in the Bolshevik ranks in the period of the October revolution? Stalin, in a speech on 19 November 1924, asked and answered this question:

"How could it happen that Trotsky, who carried such a nasty stock-in-trade on his back; found himself, after all, in the rank of the Bolsheviks during the October movement? It happened because at that time Trotsky abandoned (actually did abandon) that stock-in-trade; he hid it in the cupboard .Had he not performed that 'operation', real co-operation with him would have been impossible. The theory of the August bloc, i.e., the theory of unity with the Mensheviks, had already been shattered and thrown overboard by the revolution, for how could there be any talk about unity when an armed struggle was raging between the Bolsheviks and the Mensheviks? Trotsky had no alternative but to admit that this theory was useless.

"The same misadventure 'happened' to the theory of permanent revolution, for not a single Bolshevik contemplated the immediate seizure of power on the morrow of the February Revolution, and Trotsky could not help knowing that the Bolsheviks would not allow him, in the words of Lenin, 'to play at the seizure of power.' Trotsky had no alternative but recognise the Bolsheviks' policy of fighting for influence in the Soviets, of fighting to win over the peasantry As regards the third specific feature of Trotskyism (distrust of (he Bolshevik leaders), it had naturally to retire into the background owing to the obvious failure of the first two features.

"Under the circumstances, could Trotsky do anything else but hide his stock-in-trade in the cupboard and follow the Bolshevik; considering that he had no group of his own of any significance, and that he came to the Bolsheviks as a political individual without an army? Of course, he could not!

"What is the lesson to be learnt from this? Only one: that prolonged collaboration between the Leninists and Trotsky is possible only if the latter completely abandons his old stock-in-trade, only if he completely accepts Leninism. Trotsky writes about the lessons of October, but he forgets ... the one I have just mentioned, which prime importance for Trotskyism. Trotskyism ought to learn that lesson of October too." (*Collected Works*, Vol. 6, pp. 366-367).

Trotskyism, however, failed to learn this lesson, and its old stock-in-trade, hidden in the cupboard in the period of the October movement, was dragged into daylight once more, especially after the death of Lenin, through Trotskyist literary pronouncements aimed at undermining the Bolshevik Party principle, belittling and discrediting Lenin (albeit under the guise of praising and exalting Lenin) and asserting the correctness of the much-discredited theory of permanent revolution, which was shattered by the experience of the three Russian revolutions – ie, that of 1905 and those of February and October 1917.

On arriving in Petrograd in 1917, Trotsky affiliated to the Mezhrayontsi (inter-regional), a group that vacillated between the Bolsheviks and the

Mensheviks. In August 1917, declaring that they had no differences with the Bolsheviks, the Mezhrayontsi joined the Russian Social Democratic Labour Party (Bolsheviks). Trotsky joined the Bolsheviks with them. On joining the Bolshevik Party, quite a number of Mezhrayontsi broke with opportunism; but, as subsequent events were to reveal, for Trotsky and some of his followers, joining the Bolsheviks was only a ruse. They continued to propound their harmful and reactionary views, flout discipline and undermine the Party's organisational and ideological unity.

As Trotskyism, Ear from abandoning its old nasty stock-in-trade, on the contrary dragged it out into the light of day, it was bound, owing to its entire inner content, to become the centre and rallying point not only of the non-proletarian elements in the USSR who were then (in the 1920s and 1930s) striving to disintegrate the proletarian dictatorship, but also of the imperialist bourgeoisie seeking by a thousand means to overthrow the proletarian regime that had been ushered in by the mighty October revolution. At every crucial stage in the development of the Russian revolution and the existence of the dictatorship of the proletariat in the USSR, Trotskyism continued to maintain its reactionary anti-Bolshevik, anti-Leninist stance in matters of theory as well as organisation, cloaking it under thick layers of 'revolutionary' rhetoric.

Brest-Litovsk

In 1918 the young Soviet Republic, bereft of any army with the will and ability to fight, was fighting for its very survival through signing the Brest-Litovsk Peace Treaty with German imperialism, thus gaining a much-needed respite for the exhausted population. At a crucial moment in these negotiations, Trotsky, as the head of the Soviet delegation to the peace talks, in violation of the instructions of the Party central committee and the Soviet government, declared the unilateral withdrawal of the Soviet Republic from the war, demobilisation of the Russian Army, and he then left Brest-Litovsk on the spurious ground that "we can only be saved in the true meaning of the word by a European Revolution" (*Extraordinary Seventh Congress of the RCP(B)*).

This gave the German Command the pretext it needed for ending the armistice, mounting an offensive and obliging the Soviet government to sign "a much more humiliating peace, and the blame for this rests on those who refused to accept the former peace." (Lenin, *Political Report of the CC to the Extraordinary Seventh Congress of the RCP (B)*, 7 March 1918, *Collected Works*, Vol. 27).

Apropos the failure of the European revolution to come to maturity thus leaving the Bolshevik Revolution to solve its problems on its own, and forcing the Bolsheviks to face reality as it was rather than as they would wish it to be, Lenin admonished Trotsky and his ilk in the Party in the following terms:

"If you are unable to adapt yourself, if you are not inclined to crawl on your belly in the mud you are not a revolutionary but a chatterbox; and I propose this, not because I like it, but because we have no other road, because history has not been kind enough to bring the revolution to maturity everywhere simultaneously." (*Ibid.*)

Thus the young Soviet Republic paid a very heavy price for Trotsky's adventurism and phrase-mongering defeatism, which is the chief characteristic of his rotten theory of permanent revolution, according to which nothing good can ever come of any revolution unless it is accompanied by a world revolution.

Trade union debate

With the victorious conclusion of the Civil War of 1918-1920, as the Soviet Republic under Lenin's guidance, switched from war communism to the New Economic Policy (NEP) and embarked on a programme of economic revival and rejuvenation – of restoration of industry through an upsurge in agriculture and by drawing the workers and trade unions into active socialist construction through planned organisation and persuasion (and not coercion), Trotsky and his supporters forced on the Party a discussion on the question of trade unions (a luxury and a diversion from the work of economic construction, from the fight against famine and economic dislocation that the Party could ill afford at the time). Trotsky, the patriarch of bureaucrats, as Stalin rightly called him insisted on "tightening up the screws" and "shaking up" the trade unions, and turning the latter into state agencies, and on replacing persuasion by coercion.

The Party discussion on the trade unions resulted in the total rout of Trotsky and his supporters. When the Central Committee of the Party rejected Trotsky's Prussian sergeant's proposal, Trotsky went outside and gathered a group of his supporters with the aim of fighting against the Central Committee. So alarmed was Lenin by Trotsky's factionalism and flouting of Party discipline that he caused the 10th Party Congress (March 1921) to pass a resolution forbidding the formation of factions and disbanding existing factions forthwith. It was further stated that the "non-fulfilment of this decision of the Congress shall be followed by unconditional and immediate expulsion from the Party."

Trotsky's return to fully-fledged factionalism

This resolution was to arouse Trotsky's bitter hatred and opposition, for whenever he could not get his own way on any question, he rushed to form a Trotskyist faction within the Party, even if that meant threatening a split.

During 1921 Lenin's health began to decline. Cerebral arteriosclerosis was already blocking his blood circulation and taking its toll, with the result that this man of inexhaustible energy and drive was tiring easily, and spent most of the summer resting in the village of Gorki, not far from Moscow. The 11th Party Congress, meeting at the end of March 1922, created the new office of General Secretary, to which, one day after the conclusion of that Congress (i.e., on 3 April 1922), on Lenin's initiation and sponsorship, Stalin was appointed. On 26 May 1922, while resting in Gorki, Lenin suffered a severe stroke, which caused a partial paralysis of the right side of his body and loss of speech. He recovered from this stroke remarkably quickly and was back at his desk in early October 1922. After two further minor strokes on December 13 and 16, 1922, he suffered on March 10, 1923, a massive stroke, from which he never recovered and after which he took no further part in politics.

Following the latest stroke suffered by Lenin, Trotsky, with an eye on the leadership, stepped up his factional activity and intensified his vile and slanderous attacks on the Party leadership, its central institutions and its policy. On 8 October 1923 he sent a letter to the Central Committee, in which he asserted that the country was being inexorably led by the Party leadership to a catastrophe, to prevent which he demanded greater inner-Party democracy. Stripped of its Trotskyite verbiage, this meant the right to form factional groupings. A group of 46 followers of Trotsky also issued a manifesto – known as the Statement of 46 – to the same effect. Trotsky's letter and the Statement of 46 were discussed and condemned at a joint plenary meeting of the CC and the CCC with representatives of ten of the largest Party organisations in October 1923.

Trotsky followed his letter with a pamphlet entitled New Course, in which in addition to the demand for more Party democracy, he accused the old Bolsheviks – the Party leadership – of degeneration. He counterposed young people, especially students, to veteran Bolsheviks, declaring the former to be the barometer of the Party.

In talking about the degeneration of the 'old guard', Trotsky had used the expression "we, the old Bolsheviks," which provoked Stalin to make this observation, full of biting sarcasm:

"First, I must dispel a possible misunderstanding. As is evident..., Trotsky includes himself among the Bolshevik old guard, thereby showing readiness to take upon himself the charges that may be hurled at the old guard if it does indeed take the path of degeneration. It must be admitted that his readiness for self-sacrifice is undoubtedly a noble trait. But I must protect Trotsky from Trotsky, because, for obvious reasons, he cannot and should not bear responsibility for the possible degeneration of the principal cadres of the Bolshevik old guard..."

With more than a covert reference to Trotsky's long Menshevik past, Stalin, while admitting the possibility of degeneration of the Bolshevik old guard, goes on to add:

"Nevertheless, there are a number of elements within our Party who are capable of giving rise to a real danger of degeneration of certain ranks of our Party. I have in mind that section of the Mensheviks who joined our Party unwillingly and who have not yet got rid of their opportunist habits." (*Collected Works*, Vol. 5 p. 395).

The Thirteenth Conference of the RCP(B), held on 16-18 January 1924, strongly condemned the factionalism of Trotsky and his followers, stating that "the present opposition is not only an attempt to revise Bolshevism not only a flagrant departure from Leninism but patently a **petty-bourgeois deviation** .There is no doubt whatever that this opposition mirrors the pressure of the petty-bourgeoisie on the position of the proletarian party and its policy." (*Resolution On the Results of the Discussion and on the Petty-Bourgeois Deviation in the Party* – CPSU in Resolutions, etc. Vol. 2).

Lenin's death and Trotsky's attempt to substitute Trotskyism for Leninism

Lenin, after a further stroke on the morning of 21 January, 1924, died in the evening. Trotsky, although a newcomer to the Party, had convinced himself that he had a better claim to succeed Lenin than old, trusted and tried Bolsheviks such as Stalin. So in October 1924 Trotsky published an introduction to his collected works entitled Lessons of October, which purported to deal with the reasons for the Bolshevik victory in the October Revolution. Having made general ritual references in it to the necessity of a revolutionary party for the success of a revolution, Trotsky went on to belittle the role of the Bolshevik Party, extol his, own part in the revolution, hinting that Lenin had suddenly changed his previous position for that of Trotsky, to which fact alone was to be attributed the success of the October Revolution. He also dragged out of the cupboard his old and much-discredited theory of 'permanent revolution!, arguing that hostile collisions between the proletarian vanguard and the broad masses of the peasantry were inevitable. One gets the impression from reading his *Lessons of October* that it was Trotsky who organised the October victory.

In other words, the man who had fought against Bolshevism and Leninism for 14 long years, who had sided with the Mensheviks and liquidators to oppose the building by Lenin's Bolsheviks of the proletarian revolutionary party capable of leading the proletariat and the broad masses in seizing political power, who had spent his life opposing Lenin's theory of proletarian revolution with his absurd theory of 'permanent revolution', who had opposed the Bolshevik slogan of defeat of one's own government in the imperialist war (the first world war) with his chauvinistic slogan demanding *Neither victory nor defeat,* suddenly and providentially descended on the scene in Petersburg to rescue the revolution from the frightened and useless lot that constituted the Central Committee of the Bolshevik Party, the majority of whom, according to this fairy tale worthy of the *Arabian Nights*, were opposed to the October uprising!!

Nothing could be further from the truth. Trotsky's special role in October originated with John Reed, the author of *Ten Days that Shook the World*, who, being remote from the Bolshevik Party, had no knowledge of the secret meeting of its central committee on 23 October, 1917, and was therefore taken in by the gossip spread by people such as Sukhanov. These fairy tales about Trotsky's special role in October were later passed round and repeated in several pamphlets written by Trotskyites, including Syrkin's pamphlet on October. After Lenin's death Trotsky strongly supported these rumours in his literary pronouncements.

Since a systematic attempt was being made by Trotskyites to re- write the history of October and bring up Soviet youth on such legends, Stalin, in a speech delivered at the Plenum of the Communist Group of the AUCCTU,[3] refuted – by reference to hard facts – these *Arabian Nights* fairy tales in his characteristically devastating manner. Citing the minutes of the meeting of the Central Committee of the Bolshevik Party on 23 October 1917, he proved that the resolution on the uprising was adopted by a majority of 10 against 2; that the same meeting elected a *political* centre, called the Political Bureau, to direct the uprising, the members of the Centre being Lenin, Zinoviev, Stalin, Kamenev, Trotsky, Sokolnikov and Bubnov. Thus the Centre included even Zinoviev and Kamenev who were the only two to vote against the resolution on the uprising. This was possible in spite of the political disagreements between them because there was at that time a unity of views between these two (Zinoviev and Kamenev) and the rest of the Central Committee on such fundamental questions "as the character of the Russian revolution, the driving forces of the revolution, the role of the peasantry, the principles of Party leadership, and so forth." (Stalin, *Collected Works*, Vol. 6, p. 341). Thus the decision on the uprising was taken by the Central Committee and the Central Committee alone. Hence the political direction of the uprising was firmly in the hands of the Central Committee.

As to the legend that Trotsky played a 'special' role in that he 'inspired', and was the 'sole leader' of the October uprising – this legend was spread by Lentsner, and Stalin dealt with it as follows:

"The Trotskyites are vigorously spreading rumours that Trotsky inspired and was the sole leader of the October uprising. These rumours are being spread with exceptional zeal by the so- called editor of Trotsky's works, Lentsner. Trotsky himself, by consistently avoiding mention of the Party, the Central Committee and the Petrograd Committee of the Party, by saying nothing about the leading role of these organisations in the uprising and vigorously pushing himself forward as the central figure in the October uprising, voluntarily or involuntarily helps to spread the rumours about the special role he is supposed to have played in the uprising, I am far from denying

Trotsky's undoubtedly important role in the uprising. I must say, however, that Trotsky did not play any special role in the October uprising, nor could he do so; being chairman of the Petrograd Soviet he merely carried out the will of the appropriate Party bodies, which directed every step that Trotsky took .To philistines like Sukhanov, all this may seem strange, but the facts, the true facts, wholly and fully confirm what I say." (*Ibid*, pp. 341- 342).

Stalin then passes on to an examination of the minutes of the next Central Committee meeting held on 29 October, 1917. Apart from the members of the Central Committee, there were present at this meeting representatives of the Petrograd Committee as well as representatives of military organisations, factory committees, trade unions and the railwaymen. At this meeting Lenin's resolution on the uprising was adopted by a majority of 20 against 2, with three abstentions. At this meeting too a practical centre was elected for the organisational leadership of the uprising. To this practical centre were elected the following five: Sverdlov, Stalin, Dzerzhinksy, Bubnov and Uritsky. Let Stalin speak:

"The functions of the practical centre: to direct all the practical organs of the uprising in conformity with the directives of the Central Committee. Thus, as you see, something terrible happened at this meeting of the Central Committee, i.e., 'strange to relate', the Inspirer, the 'chief figure', the 'sole leader' of the uprising, Trotsky, was not elected to the practical centre, which was called upon to direct the uprising. How is this to be reconciled with the current opinion about Trotsky's special role? Is not all this somewhat 'strange', as Sukhanov, or the Trotskyites, would say? And yet strictly speaking there is nothing strange about it for neither in the Party, nor in the October uprising did Trotsky play any **special** role, nor could he do so, for he was a relatively new man in our Party in the period of October. He, like all the responsible workers, merely carried out the will of the Central Committee and of its organs. Who-ever is familiar with the mechanics of Bolshevik Party leadership will have no difficulty in understanding that it could not be otherwise; it would have been enough for Trotsky to go against the will of the Central Committee to have been deprived of all influence on the course of events. This talk about Trotsky's special role is a legend that is being spread by obliging 'Party' gossips.[4]

"This, of course, does not mean that the October uprising did not have its inspirer. it did have its inspirer and leader, but this was Lenin, and none other than Lenin, that same Lenin whose resolution the Central Committee adopted when deciding the question of the uprising, that same Lenin who, in spite of what Trotsky says, was not prevented by being in hiding from being the actual inspirer of the uprising. It is foolish and ridiculous to attempt now, by gossip about Lenin having been in hiding to obscure the indubitable fact that the inspirer of the uprising was the leader of the Party, V.I. Lenin.

"Such are the facts." (*Collected Works*, Vol. 6, pp 342-344.)

Continues Stalin:

"Granted, we are told but it cannot be denied that Trotsky fought well in the period of October. Yes, that is true, Trotsky did, indeed, fight well in October, but Trotsky was not the only one who fought well in the period of October. Even people like the Left Socialist-Revolutionaries, who then stood side by side with the Bolsheviks, also fought well, In general I "must say that in the period of a victorious uprising when the enemy is isolated and the uprising is growing; it is not difficult to fight well. At such moments even backward people become heroes.

"The proletarian struggle is not however, an uninterrupted advance, an unbroken chain of victories. The proletarian struggle also has its trials, its defeats. The genuine revolutionary is not one who displays courage in the period of a victorious uprising; but one who, while fighting well during the victorious advance of the revolution, also displays courage when the revolution is in retreat when the proletariat suffers defeat, who does not lose his head and does not funk when the revolution suffers reverses, when the enemy "achieves success; who does not become panic-stricken or give way to despair when the revolution is in a period of retreat The Left Socialist-Revolutionaries did not fight badly in the period of October, and they supported the Bolsheviks. But who does not know that those 'brave' fighters became panic-stricken in the period of Brest when the advance of German imperialism drove them to despair and hysteria. It is a very sad but indubitable fact that Trotsky, who fought well in the period of October, did not in the period of Brest in the period when the revolution suffered temporary reverses, possess the courage to display sufficient staunchness at that difficult moment and to refrain from following in the footsteps of the Left Socialist-Revolutionaries. Beyond question; that moment was a difficult one; one had to display exceptional courage and imperturbable coolness not to be dismayed, to retreat in good time, to accept peace in good time, to withdraw the proletarian army out of range of the blows of German imperialism; to preserve the peasant reserves and, after obtaining a respite in this way, to strike at the enemy with renewed force. Unfortunately, Trotsky was found to lack this courage and revolutionary staunchness at that difficult moment.

"In Trotsky's opinion, the principal lesson of the proletarian revolution is 'not to funk' during October. That is wrong; for Trotsky's assertion contains only a particle of the truth about the lessons of the revolution. The whole truth about the lessons of the proletarian revolution is not to funk, not only when the revolution is advancing but also when it is retreat when the enemy is gaining the upper hand and the revolution is suffering reverses. The revolution did not end with October. October was only the beginning of the proletarian revolution. It is bad to funk when the tide of insurrection is rising but it is worse to funk when the revolution is passing through severe trials after power has been captured. To retain power on the morrow of the revolution is no less important that to capture power." (*Ibid*. pp. 344-345).

Stalin asked the question: "For what purpose did Trotsky need all these legends about October and the preparation for October, about Lenin and the Party of Lenin? What is the purpose of Trotsky's new literary pronouncements against the Party?..." (*Ibid*. p.363)

By way of an answer, Stalin continues:

"Trotsky asserts that all this is needed for the purpose of 'studying' October. But is it not possible to study October without giving another kick at the Party and its leader Lenin? What sort of a 'history' of October is it that begins and ends with attempts to discredit the chief leader of the October uprising to discredit the Party, which organised and carried through the uprising?... **That** is not the way to study October. **That** is not the way to write the history of October. Obviously, there is a different 'design' here, and everything goes to show that this 'design' is that Trotsky by his literary pronouncements is making another (yet another!) attempt to create the conditions for substituting Trotskyism for Leninism. Trotsky needs 'desperately' to discredit the Party, and its cadres who carried through the uprising in order, after discrediting the Party, to proceed to discredit Leninism. And it is necessary for him to discredit Leninism in order to drag in Trotskyism as the 'sole' 'proletarian' (don't laugh!) ideology. All this, of course (oh, of course!) under the flag of Leninism, so that the dragging operation may be performed 'as painlessly as possible'.

"That is the essence of Trotsky's latest literary pronouncements." (*Ibid*. pp. 363-364).

Trotskyism – a rallying point for counter-revolution

Stalin went on to conclude that the danger was "... that Trotskyism, owing to its entire inner content stands every chance of becoming the centre and rallying point of the non-proletarian elements who are striving to weaken to disintegrate the proletarian dictatorship," in view of which it was "the duty of the Party to **bury Trotskyism** as an ideological trend." (*Ibid*. p. 373).

In later years Trotsky himself was obliged to admit that "in the wake of this vanguard [i.e., the Trotskyist opposition] there dragged the tail end of all sorts of dissatisfied, ill-equipped and even chagrined careerists," adding, however, that the opposition had managed to free itself from "its accidental and uninvited fellow wayfarers." On the contrary, as the contents of the pages that follow reveal, it is precisely the non-proletarian elements, with their irreconcilable hostility to the proletarian dictatorship, their striving for the disintegration of the proletarian dictatorship, who supported the Trotskyist opposition in the USSR and who continued to support him abroad after his expulsion from the Soviet Union. It is precisely the same type of person who has since those times rallied around Trotskyism, driven by an innate hatred of Marxism-Leninism and of the dictatorship of the proletariat.

Even the Trotskyite Deutscher is compelled to say. 'Outside the party, formless revolutionary frustration mingled with distinctly counter-revolutionary trends Since the ruling group had singled out Trotsky as a target for attack he automatically attracted the spurious sympathy of many who had hitherto hated him. As he made his appearance in the streets of Moscow [in. the spring of 1924], he was spontaneously applauded by crowds in which idealist communists rubbed shoulders with Mensheviks Social Revolutionaries; and the new bourgeoisie of the NEP, by all those indeed who, for diverse reasons hoped for a change [i.e., for the disintegration of the proletarian dictatorship through the weakening and disintegration of the Bolshevik Party]" (Isaac Deutscher, *Stalin*, Pelican, 1966, p. 279).

At its plenary meeting held on 17-20 January, 1925, the Central Committee of the RCP(B) characterised Trotskyism as a variety of Menshevism" and Trotsky's ceaseless attacks on Bolshevism as an attempt to substitute Trotskyism for Leninism. This meeting resolved to remove Trotsky from the office of Chairman of the Revolutionary Military Council of the USSR, and he was "warned in the most emphatic term that membership of the Bolshevik Party demands real, not verbal subordination to Party discipline and total and unconditional renunciation of any attacks on the ideals of Leninism "

Emergence of the New Opposition

After the above meeting pronounced against Trotsky and warned that his splittist activity and anti Leninist propaganda was incompatible with Party membership, Trotsky retreated for a while, awaiting his chance This chance came when Zinoviev and Kamenev – two old Bolsheviks – frightened by difficulties and overcome by defeatism, went into opposition after the 14th Party Conference (April 1925) affirmed the possibility of building socialism, in the USSR. Being incorrigible defeatists and sceptics, Zinoviev and Kamenev denied the possibility of building socialism in the Soviet Union, and in this way found common ground with pessimism, scepticism and defeatism personified, namely, Trotsky, the author of the theory of 'permanent revolution', the epitome of hopelessness.

The New Opposition (as it was called), led by Zinoviev and Kamenev, launched 'vicious attacks on the Party's Leninist line (on the possibility of building socialism) at the 14th Congress of the Party, winch opened in December 1925. After suffering a crushing defeat at that Congress, the New Opposition, headed by Zinoviev and Kamenev (who had until only recently been -seeking to remove Trotsky from the leadership and whom Trotsky, in turn, had been seeking to eliminate from the leadership of the Party) openly embraced Trotskyism. Thus emerged an anti-Party opposition bloc, to which flocked the remnants of the various opposition groups previously squashed by the Party – all motivated by their hatred of, and opposition to, the Party's policy of strengthening the proletarian dictatorship and building socialism in the USSR.

The leaders of this opposition, Trotsky, Zinoviev and Kamenev, "granting each other mutual amnesty," as Stalin put it, and using as an occasion and a pretext the collapse of the British General Strike (that they blamed on the leadership of the Bolshevik Party for having allegedly failed to give leadership and guidance to the British workers), produced their platform, written by Trotsky, which was presented in part to the Plenum of the Central Committee on 6-9 April 1926, and in full to the meeting of July 14-23 1926. In flagrant breach of Party discipline, the opposition organised demonstrations in factories, demanding full discussion of their platform. The communist workers vehemently denounced the opposition leaders and made them leave these meetings. Faced with this humiliating defeat, the opposition leaders beat a retreat and sent a statement, on 16 October 1926, in which they confessed their errors and promised to desist in future from their factional activity against the Party. In the words of Ian Grey:

"Appalled by their own temerity and recklessness, the six leaders – Trotsky, Zinoviev, Kamenev, Pyatakov, Sokolnikov and Evdakimov – confessed their guilt in a public declaration and swore not to pursue factional activity in future. They also denounced their own left-wing supporters in the Comintern and the Workers' Opposition group." (Ian Grey, *Stalin – Man of History*, Abacus, 1982, pp. 213-214).

Formation of an illegal party

The opposition's statement of October, 1926, turned out to be totally insincere and thoroughly hypocritical. As a matter of fact the opposition had formed an illegal party of its own, with a separate system of membership, district committees, and a centre. The illegal party, with a secret illegal printing press, held secret meetings at which the opposition's factional platform, and the tactics to be adopted against the Bolshevik Party, were discussed – all this in violation of the decisions of the 10th Party Congress banning the formation and continuation of separate factions within the Party.

In October 1926, the Plenum of the Central Committee, sitting jointly with the Central Control Commission, issued a severe warning to the leaders of the opposition, removing Trotsky from the Politburo and Kamenev from his candidate membership of this body. Zinoviev was removed from the Comintern.

The Fifteenth All-Union Party Conference (Oct-Nov 1926) characterised the Trotsky-Zinoviev opposition as a Menshevik deviation in the Party, issuing the warning that further development in the direction of Menshevism would lead to the opposition's expulsion from the Party.

At the beginning of 1927 the opposition renewed its attack on the policy of the Comintern vis-à-vis the Chinese revolution, blaming the Comintern and the CPSU for the reverses of the Chinese revolution. Taking advantage of the internal difficulties, as well as of the deterioration in the international position of the USSR, the opposition yet again came out with the so-called 'platform of 83'. Renewing their slander against the Party, the opposition claimed in this platform that the Soviet government was intending to abolish the monopoly of foreign trade and grant political fights to the kulaks. Such slanders could not but encourage the kulaks and imperialism alike in putting pressure on the Soviet government in an attempt to wrest precisely such concessions from the Soviet government. In addition, the opposition dema-gogically demanded greater freedom in the Party, which it understood to mean the freedom to form factions and to "indulge in unparalleled abuse and impermissible vilification of the Central Committee, CPSU(B) and the ECCI. They complain of the 'regime' within the Comintern and the CPSU(B). Essentially, what they want is freedom to disorganise the Comintern and the CPSU(B)..." (Stalin, *Collected Works*, Vol. 9, p. 317).

Trotskyism's struggle against 'Stalinism'
– a continuation of the struggle against Leninism

What the Trotskyite opposition was fighting against was the regime es-tablished by the 10th congress under the guidance of Lenin – a regime de-signed to strengthen the dictatorship of the proletariat through unity and iron discipline within the Bolshevik Party by outlawing factionalism. The under-lying principles of the regime established by the 10th Congress were that "while inner-Party democracy is operated and businesslike criticism of the Party's defects and mistakes is permitted no factionalism whatsoever is per-mitted, and all factionalism must be abandoned on pain of expulsion from the party.," (Stalin, *The Political Completion of the Russian Opposition, Collected Works,* Vol. 10, p. 166).

"I assert", said Stalin, "that the Trotskyites had already started their fight against the Leninist regime in the Party in Lenin's time, and that the fight the Trotskyites are now [i.e., September 19271 waging is a continuation of the fight against the regime in the Party which they were already waging in Lenin's time." (*Ibid.*)

As the opposition's platform drew no support from the workers, it re-treated again and handed another declaration to the Central Committee, on 8 August 1927, in which they promised yet again to cease their factional activ-ity, only to violate it a month later.

As the preparations got under way in September 1927 for the Fifteenth Party Congress, the opposition drew up the third statement of its aims and policies. An end had to be put to the opposition's factionalism, its disorgan-ising activity and the charade of repeated violations of its hypocritical decla-ration of admission of guilt and promises to cease factional activity. So, at the end of October 1927, the Central Committee in a joint meeting with the

Central Control Commission, expelled Trotsky and Zinoviev from the Central Committee, deciding further to submit all the documents relating to the factional activity of the Trotskyite opposition to the Fifteenth Congress for consideration by the latter.

It is worth recalling that during the Party discussion preceding the Fifteenth Party Congress, 724,000 members voted for the Leninist policy of the Central Committee, while a derisory 4,000 votes were cast for the platform of the Trotskyite-Zinovievite opposition bloc, that is, half of one per cent of the membership that took part in this debate.

Why did the opposition fail?

The opposition failed to get any support in the Party organisations, for its line was that of utter bankruptcy the line of wanting to supplant Leninism by Trotskyism, while the Party wished faithfully to pursue the line of Leninism – that of revolutionary Bolshevism.

"How, then," asked Stalin, "are we to explain the fact that notwithstanding his oratorical skill, notwithstanding his will to lead, notwithstanding his abilities, Trotsky was thrown out of the leadership of the great Party which is called the CPSU(B)?" He went on to answer: "The reason is that the opposition intended to **replace** Leninism with Trotskyism, to **'improve'** Leninism by means Of Trotskyism. But the Party want to remain faithful to Leninism in spite of all the various artifices of the down-at-heel aristocrats in the Party. That is the root cause why the Party, which has made three revolutions, found it necessary to turn its back on Trotsky and on the opposition as a whole." (*Collected Works,* Vol. 10, p. 165).

Speaking at the Fifteenth Congress of the Party, Stalin returned to this question again. "How could it happen that the Party as a whole, and after it the working class as well so thoroughly isolated the opposition? After all the opposition is headed by well-known people with well-known names, people who know how to advertise themselves..., people who are not afflicted with modesty and who are able to blow their own trumpets, to make the most of their wares.

"It happened because the leading group of the opposition proved to be a group of petty-bourgeois intellectuals divorced from life, divorced from the revolution, divorced from the Party, from the working class." (Stalin, *ibid.* p. 345).

From factionalism within the Party to counter-revolutionary struggle against the Soviet regime

Faced with utter defeat within the Party, bankrupt politically and isolated from the Party membership, the Trotskyite-Zinovievite bloc switched over from factional activity within the Party to anti-Soviet and counter-revolutionary struggle against the Bolshevik regime, attracting in the process all the anti-Soviet elements to their camp.

On 7 November, 1927, the tenth anniversary of the October Revolution, Trotsky and Zinoviev organised anti-Party demonstrations in Moscow and Leningrad. Poorly attended, these counter-revolutionary demonstrations were easily dispersed by the demonstrators of the working class under the leadership of the CPSU.

By its November 7 actions the opposition had given full proof of its conversion into a counter-revolutionary force openly hostile to the proletarian dictatorship in the USSR. Having infringed all the norms and rules of Party life, the Trotskyites now embarked upon a career of violating state laws which in due course led them to murder, sabotage, wrecking and, finally, to an alliance with fascism.

On 14 November, 1927, the Central Committee expelled Trotsky and Zinoviev from the Party, while other members of their group were removed from the Central Committee and the Central Control Commission.

The Fifteenth Congress of the Party (December 1927), noting that the opposition had ideologically broken with Leninism, had degenerated into Menshevism, had adopted the path of capitulation to international imperialism and the internal bourgeoisie and had become an instrument of struggle against the dictatorship of the proletariat, enthusiastically endorsed these expulsions. Moreover it expelled in addition a further 75 members of the Trotsky-Zinoviev bloc, as well as 15 Democratic Centralists. Further, the Congress instructed Party organisations to purge their ranks of incorrigible Trotskyites and take steps to re-educate the rank-and-file members of the opposition in the spirit of Leninism.

After the Congress many ordinary members of the opposition recognised their errors, broke with Trotskyism and were restored to Party membership. In January 1928 Trotsky was exiled to Alma-Ata in Central Asia (Kazakhstan). Even there he continued clandestinely to indulge in his anti-Party, anti-Soviet activity. Consequently, in January 1929 he was expelled from the Soviet Union.

Since the opposition intended little by little to switch the Bolshevik Party from the Leninist path to that of Trotskyism, and since the Party wanted to remain a Leninist Party, it was only natural that the Party turned its back on the opposition and raised ever higher the banner of Leninism. This alone explains why, as Stalin put it, "yesterday's leaders of the Party have now become renegades." (*Collected Works*, Vol. 10, p. 199).

Not personal factors but departure from Leninism is the cause of Trotskyism's failure

Instead of grasping this truth, the Trotskyite opposition in its day, and the Trotskyites ever since then, have explained the opposition's defeat by personal factors. This is how Stalin described the far-reaching historical roots of Trotsky's fight against Bolshevism and the reasons for the failure and bankruptcy of the opposition's line:

"The opposition thinks that its defeat can be 'explained' by the personal factor, by Stalin's rudeness... That is too cheap an explanation. It is an incantation, not an explanation. Trotsky has been fighting Leninism since 1904. From 1904 until the February revolution in 1917 he hung around the Mensheviks desperately fighting Lenin's Party all the time. During that period Trotsky suffered a number of defeats at the hand of Lenin's Party- Why? Perhaps Stalin's rudeness was to blame? But Stalin was not yet the secretary of the Central Committee at that time; he was not abroad, but in Russia, fighting tsarism underground, whereas the struggle between Trotsky and Lenin raged abroad. So what has Stalin's rudeness got to do with it?

"During the period from the October Revolution to 1922, Trotsky, already a member of the Bolshevik Party, managed to make two 'grand' sorties against Lenin and his Party: in 1918 – on the question of the Brest Peace; and in 1921 – on the trade-union question. Both those sorties ended in Trotsky being defeated. Why? Perhaps Stalin's rudeness was to blame here? But at that time Stalin was not yet the secretary of the Central Committee. The secretarial posts were then occupied by notorious Trotskyists. So what has Stalin's rudeness got to do with it?

"Later, Trotsky made a number of fresh sorties against the Party (1923, 1924, 1926, 1927) and each sortie ended in Trotsky suffering a fresh defeat.

"Is it not obvious from all this that Trotsky's fight against the Leninist Party has deep, far-reaching historical roots? Is it not obvious from this that the struggle the Party is now waging against Trotskyism is a continuation of the struggle that the Party, headed by Lenin, waged from 1904 onwards?

"Is it not obvious from all this that the attempts of the Trotskyists to replace Leninism by Trotskyism are the chief cause of the failure and bankruptcy of the entire line of the opposition?

"Our Party was born and grew up in the storm of revolutionary battles. It is not a party that grew up in a period of peaceful development. For that very reason it is rich in revolutionary traditions and does not make a fetish of its leaders. At one time Plekhanov was the most popular man in the Party. More than that he was the founder of the Party, and his popularity was incomparably greater than that of Trotsky or Zinoviev. Nevertheless, in spite of that the Party turned away from Plekhanov as soon as he began to depart from Marxism and go over to opportunism. Is it surprising, then, that people who are not so 'great, people like Trotsky and Zinoviev, found themselves at the tail of the Party after they began to depart from Leninism?" (*Collected Works*, Vol. 10, pp 199-201).

Just as the struggle waged against Trotskyism by the Bolshevik Party headed by Stalin from 1924 onwards was a continuation of the struggle that the Party headed by Lenin had waged from 1903 onwards, equally Trotsky's fight against the Bolshevik Party headed by Stalin was a continuation of the struggle that Trotskyism waged against the Bolshevik Party when it was headed by Lenin. Lenin had been the chief target of Trotsky's vilifications from 1903 to 1917. After the death of Lenin, Stalin came to occupy this honourable position, became the chief target of the opposition's attack. This was because Stalin, by faithfully defending and carrying forward the Leninist fine, became the most representative spokesman of the Bolshevik Party and in that capacity drew the wrath of the opposition in its repeated, if unsuccessful, attempts to substitute Trotskyism for Leninism. It was not a case of the allegedly Leninist Trotsky fighting against an allegedly outside usurper, Stalin, as is put out in Trotskyite fairy tales; on the contrary, it was the staunch and indefatigable Leninist (Stalin) who brilliantly continued the successful Leninist assault on the anti-Bolshevik and petty-bourgeois ideology of Trotskyism. This alone explains Trotskyism's hatred of Joseph St" the very mention of whose name causes Trotskyite gentry to foam at the mouth- This is how Stalin described the opposition's hatred for him:

"First of all about the personal factor. You have heard here how assiduously the oppositionists hurl abuse at Stalin, abuse him with all their might. The reason why the main attacks were directed against Stalin is because Stalin knows all the opposition's tricks better, perhaps, than some of our comrades do, and it is not easy, I dare say, to fool him. So they strike their blows primarily at Stalin. Well, let them hurt abuse to their hearts' content.

"And what is Stalin? Stalin is only a minor figure. Take Lenin. Who does not know that at the time of the August bloc the opposition, headed by Trotsky, waged an even more scurrilous campaign of slander against Lenin? Listen to Trotsky, for example.

"'The wretched squabbling systematically provoked by Lenin, that old hand at the game, that professional exploiter of all that is backward in the Russian labour movement, seems like a senseless obsession' (See *Trotsky's 'Letter to Chkeidze', April 1913*).

"Note the language, comrades! Note the language! It is Trotsky writing. And writing about Lenin.

"Is it surprising, then, that Trotsky, who wrote in such an ill-mannered way about the great Lenin, whose shoe-laces he was not worthy of tying, should now hurl abuse at one of Lenin's numerous pupils – Comrade Stalin?

"More than that. I think the opposition does me honour by venting all its hatred against Stalin. That is as it should be. I think it would be strange and offensive if the opposition, which is trying to wreck the Party, were to praise Stalin, who is defending the fundamentals of the Leninist Party principle." (*Collected Works*, Vol. 10, pp. 177-178).

Trotsky's regular predictions of doom

Proceeding from the unscientific and pessimistic, not to say anti-Leninist, theory of 'permanent revolution', which was refuted by the experience of the three Russian revolutions and by all further social development in the USSR and elsewhere, Trotsky could, and did, predict nothing but doom. The underlying theme and purpose of all his statements between 1923 and 1940 was to deny all possibility of building socialism in the USSR and thus to undermine the confidence of the Soviet proletariat in building a new society by its own efforts if the world revolution failed to come to its rescue. This was accompanied by vicious attacks on the only guarantee for the successes of the USSR during this epoch-making period of particular difficulty and particular achievement, namely the Leninist leadership of the Party and state of the proletarian dictatorship. Of course these attacks were always hidden under a guise of attacking the 'bureaucratic state apparatus', or 'Stalinist bureaucracy, with the alleged desire to improve matters. And when the oft-predicted disaster did not happen, this only provided Trotsky with an occasion to report on invented widespread disaster, disillusionment and demoralisation as a means of bringing about the fulfilment of his jeremiads.

Trotsky's 'New Course' predicts degeneration of the Party

In 1923, at the time of the New Economic Policy (NEP), Trotsky predicted immediate doom for the proletarian dictatorship through the "degeneration of the state apparatus in a bourgeois direction." In his *New Course*, written in 1923, he claimed that "Bureaucratism has reached an excessive and truly alarming development." This is how he predicted the restoration of capitalism through the NEP, claiming that quantity would at a certain stage be transformed into quality:

"...The rapid development of private capital... would show that private capital is interposing itself more and more between the workers' state and the peasantry, is acquiring an economic and therefore a political influence... [S]uch a rupture between Soviet industry and agriculture, between the proletariat and the peasantry, would constitute a grave danger for the proletarian revolution, a symptom of the possibility of the triumph of the counterrevolution.

"What are the political paths by which the victory of the counterrevolution might come if the economic hypothesis just set forth were to be realised?... [T]he political process would assume in the main the character of the degeneration of the state apparatus in a bourgeois direction... If private capital in creased rapidly and succeeded in fusing with the peasantry, the active counter-revolutionary tendencies directed against the Communist Party would then probably prevail...

"The counter-revolutionary tendencies can find a support among the kulaks, the middlemen, the retailers, the concessionaires, in a word, among elements much more capable of surrounding the state apparatus than the Party itself...

...[T]he negative social phenomena we have just enumerated and which now nurture bureaucratisation could place the revolution in peril should they continue to develop... bureaucratism in the state and party apparatus is the expression of the most vexatious tendencies inherent in our situation, of the defects and deviations in our work which... might sap the basis of the revolution... Quantity will at a certain stage be transformed into quality." (Chapter 4).

In all this, Trotsky forgets completely the role of the dictatorship of the proletariat. Of course, the introduction of the NEP did unleash capitalist elements, in the countryside in particular; of course it was a partial return to capitalism. All that was known to the author of the NEP, Vladimir Ilyich Lenin. But there was no other way of transition from war communism to socialism except through the NEP even though the latter, by unleashing capitalist elements in the countryside, carried the danger of capitalist restoration. This danger, however, this possibility of capitalist restoration, could never be realised as long as the proletarian dictatorship exercised its iron rule over hostile capitalist classes – kulaks and traders. That is why Lenin called for the maximum strengthening of the dictatorship of the proletariat. This, in turn, could only be done through unity of will and iron discipline in the ruling Bolshevik Party. That is why he caused the Tenth Party Congress to pass the resolution, written by himself, calling for existing factions within the Party to be disbanded forthwith, for the formation of new factions in the future to be banned, and declaring that non-compliance with this resolution by anyone would result in their immediate expulsion from the Party. Trotsky for his part consistently undermined the proletarian dictatorship by his vicious attacks on the leadership of the Party, his denigration of the Party and state apparatus in the USSR, and by flouting all norms and discipline of the Bolshevik Party.

Failure of Trotsky's predictions

Notwithstanding Trotskyist sabotage, Trotsky's predictions did not come true, thanks to the Leninist leadership of the Party and the state during this very difficult period. Instead NEP Russia was actually transformed into a mighty socialist USSR that then went on to achieve the crowning glory of defeating the mighty Nazi war machine almost single-handedly. As the "degeneration", "initiative-killing bureaucratism", "ossification", "estrangement" and "morbid uneasiness" predicted by Trotsky failed to materialise and the USSR began to be transformed through the collectivisation and industrialisation drive of the Five-Year Plans, Trotsky intensified his attacks on the USSR and the leadership of the Bolshevik Party – revealing in the process his true hideous features as a market socialist, i.e., as a bourgeois socialist of the social-democratic variety.

Contemptible and cowardly capitulator

In 1933, Trotsky published his pamphlet Soviet Economy in Danger, in which he came out in opposition to this second assault on capitalism, i.e., the assault mounted through socialist industrialisation and collectivisation – both measures of world revolutionary historic significance. He declared that the "correct and economically sound collectivisation, at a given stage, **should not lead to the elimination of the NEP** but to the **gradual reorganisation of its methods.**" (p. 32).

In other words, no attempt should be made to eliminate capitalism in general, and capitalism in the countryside in particular.

Gorbachev style, pretending to stand for some sort of control of the market, Trotsky's method of controlling the market is to leave it to the market to control itself!

"The regulation of the market," he says, "itself must depend upon the tendencies that are brought about through its medium." (p. 30).

Every revolutionary giant stride forward of the Soviet economy at that time, because outside the market, is portrayed by this high priest of market socialism as disorder and "economic chaos." He says:

"By eliminating the market and installing instead Asiatic bazaars the bureaucracy has created... the conditions for the most barbaric gyrations of prices and consequently has placed a mine under commercial calculations. As a result economic chaos has been redoubled." (p. 34).

Trotsky, who in December 1925, at the 14th Party Congress of the CPSU, had tried to force on the Party the policy of immediate collectivisation of the peasantry, when the conditions necessary for such collectivisation were totally lacking, this same Trotsky in 1933, when collectivisation was well on the way to completion, comes out in opposition to the policy of liquidating the kulaks as a class, demanding instead the establishment of "a policy of severely restricting the exploiting tendencies of the kulaks." (p. 47).

In other words, capitalism must not be eliminated in the countryside.

Praying for miracles Trotsky declares: "Commodities must be adapted to human needs..." Trotsky's position amounts to this: 'Economic accounting is unthinkable without market relations.' In view of this, it is hardly surprising that Trotsky came to the conclusion that: "It is necessary to put off the Second Five-Year Plan. Away with shrieking enthusiasm!" (p. 41).

No wonder then that Stalin, in his Report to the 17th Party Congress (26

January 1934) made the following observation on the Trotskyist programme:

"We have always said that the 'Lefts' are in fact Rights who mask their Rightness by Left phrases. Now the 'Lefts' themselves confirm the correctness of our statement. Take last year's issues of the Trotskyist 'Bulletin. What do Messieurs the Trotskyists demand, what do they write about in what does their 'Left' programme find expression? They demand: **the dissolution of the state farms,** on the grounds that they do not pay, **the dissolution of the majority of the collective farms,** on the grounds that they are fictitious, the **abandonment of the policy of eliminating the kulaks, reversion to the policy of concessions, and the leasing to concessionaires of a number of our industrial enterprises,** on the grounds that they do not pay.

"There you have the programme of these contemptible cowards and capitulators – their counter-revolutionary programme for restoring capitalism in the USSR!

"What difference is there between this programme and that of the extreme Rights? Clearly, there is none. It follows that the Lefts' have openly associated themselves with the counter-revolutionary programme of the Rights in order to enter into a bloc with them and to wage a joint struggle against the Party." (Stalin, *Collected Works*, Vol. 13, pp. 370-371.

Trotsky's anti-Soviet diatribes are grist to the imperialist mill

Although bourgeois economics learnt nothing from Trotsky's Soviet Economy in Danger, seeing as he had but repeated, in a clumsy way, what had been said a decade earlier by bourgeois economists such as Von Mises and Brutzkus, it was nevertheless extensively quoted in the imperialist press by the bourgeois critics of socialist construction, for it enabled them to stress that their 'objective' and 'impartial' critiques of socialism, and their dogma that it was impossible for society to free itself of the market, were fully accepted by this 'old Bolshevik'. (For a fuller treatment of this subject, the reader is referred to chapter 11 of my book *Perestroika – the Complete Collapse of Revisionism*).

Trotsky's diatribes against the Soviet regime were grasped with alacrity by the German and Italian fascists: "See, my friends, " said Goebbels to the German socialists and communists, "what Trotsky is saying about the Soviet state. It is no longer a Socialist State but a state dominated by a parasitic bureaucracy, living on the Russian people." (see Appendix 2) These and similar arguments, broadcast by the fascists as well as other imperialist states, were designed to weaken both the faith the masses might have in the USSR as well as their faith in themselves, in their capacity to build a new life for themselves. These Trotskyist arguments were, and continue to be, seized upon by the opponents of communism in the Labour movement as well as by the radical petty-bourgeois intelligentsia. Trotskyism thus performed, and continues to perform, the function of confusing and disarming the working-class movement politically and ideologically.

Flying in the face of all reality, ignoring the developments in socialist construction in the USSR, Trotsky continued to predict disaster and to advocate the overthrow of the 'Stalinist bureaucracy' – a euphemism for the Leninist leadership of the Bolshevik Party and the Soviet state – in other words, the overthrow of the dictatorship of the proletariat. in an article written in October 1933, Trotsky predicted the restoration of capitalism if 'Stalinist bureaucracy' continued to hold sway:

"The further unhindered development of bureaucratism must lead inevitably to the cessation of economic and cultural growth, to a terrible social crisis and to the downward plunge of the entire society. But this would imply not only the collapse of the proletarian dictatorship but also the end of bureaucratic domination. In place of the workers' state would come not 'social bureaucratic' but capitalist relations." (*The Class Nature of the Soviet State*).

In February 1935 Trotsky predicted the "inevitable collapse of the Stalinist political regime" and its replacement by fascist-capitalist counterrevolution", unless the removal of the Soviet regime came "as a conscious act of the proletarian vanguard," to wit, the same Trotskyist counter-revolutionaries who denied the very possibility of building socialism in the first place, who tried to put every obstacle (albeit unsuccessfully) in the way of socialist construction, who hand in hand with the imperialist bourgeoisie slandered the Soviet state and Bolshevik Party leadership, who belittled and denigrated every single achievement of socialist industry, agriculture, science, technology and the arts and who ended up by being allies and tools of German and Japanese fascism!! These very contemptible cowards and counter-revolutionaries, these ardent advocates of the programme of capitalist restoration, in the topsy-turvy world of Trotskyist make-believe and intrigue, convince themselves that they are the 'proletarian vanguard'! At the same time we are told by Trotsky that the Bolshevik Party which, following the Leninist line, not only believes in the possibility of building socialism in the USSR but is actually accomplishing it successfully in the face of internal and external difficulties and foes, is a regime of 'Bonapartism' which is bound to make way for 'counter-revolution' unless its removal comes about at the hands of the counter-revolutionary Trotskyists who have awarded themselves the title of "proletarian vanguard"!

"The inevitable collapse of the Stalinist political regime will lead to the establishment of Soviet democracy only in the event that the removal of Bonapartism comes as the conscious act of the proletarian vanguard In all other cases, in place of Stalinism there could only come the fascist-capitalist counterrevolution". (Trotsky, *The Workers' State, Thermidor and Bonapartism*).

Trotsky acknowledges socialist achievements as a means of gaining credibility

By the end of the Second Five-Year plan, however, even the blind could not fail to see the gigantic, truly heroic and world- historic achievements of socialist construction. Even intelligent representatives of imperialism began to make admissions of the achievements of socialism in all walks of life of the USSR – the only country to have achieved full employment while the capitalist world was reeling under the hammer blows of recession. Trotsky was in danger of being discredited because of the crying discrepancy between Soviet reality and Trotsky's description of it. So Trotsky, that most anti-Soviet of all anti-Soviets, in order to gain some credibility, was compelled to write almost effusively of the gains of socialism in the USSR, again, of course, merely as a prelude to a further scurrilous campaign of lies and slander against the Soviet regime. In his *Revolution Betrayed* (1933), he writes:

"Gigantic achievements in industry, enormously promising beginnings in agriculture, an extraordinary growth of the old industrial cities and a building of new ones, a rapid increase of the number of workers, a rise in cultural level and cultural demands – such are the indubitable results of the October revolution...

"Socialism has demonstrated its fight to victory, not in the pages of 'Das Kapital' but in an industrial arena comprising a sixth part of the earth's surface – not in the language of dialectics, but in the language of steel cement; and electricity ... a backward country has achieved in less than ten years successes unexampled in history.

"This also ends the quarrel with the reformists in the workers' movement. Can we compare for one moment their mouse-like fussing with the titanic work accomplished by this people aroused to a new life by revolution?..." (p. 16).

Thus quite mysteriously, and without any explanation let alone a correction or an apology from Trotsky, we find that the "smug, negative, disdainful cliquish, bureaucratic apparatus," characterised on the one hand by "inertia" and on the other by "antagonistic violence towards criticism," staffed with only "careerists and political hangers-on" who are so divorced from reality as to be in danger of losing support of the masses and forfeiting state dominance to the "counter-revolutionary tendencies" among "retailers, middlemen... and kulaks – this bureaucratic apparatus", i.e., the leadership of the Bolshevik Party and the Soviet state, has somehow risen to the occasion and organised "ten years of successes unexampled in history."!

Normally Trotskyism paints a picture of the Soviet people being ordered about and herded around by the 'Stalinist bureaucracy', meekly and sullenly accepting their fate. – Yet in some pages of this book, which are characteristically contradicted by some other pages in the same book, Trotsky describes the enthusiasm with which the Soviet youth plunged into economic, cultural and artistic activity, in the following glowing terms:

"To be sure, the youth are very active in the sphere of economics. In the Soviet Union there are now 1.2 million Communist Youth in the collective farms. Hundreds of thousands of members of the Communist Youth have been mobilised during recent years for construction work timber work coal mining. gold production; for work in the Arctic, Sakhalin, or in Amur where the new town of Komsomolsk is in process of construction. The new generation is putting out shock brigades, champion workers, Stakhanovites, foremen; under administrators. The youth are studying and a considerable part of them are studying assiduously. They are as active, if not more so, in the sphere of athletics in its most daring or war-like forms such as parachute jumping and marksmanship. The enterprising and audacious are going on all kinds of dangerous expeditions.

"'The better part of our youth,' said recently the well-known polar explorer, Schmidt, 'are eager to work where difficulties await them.' This is undoubtedly true...

"... [I]t would be a crude slander against the youth to portray them as controlled exclusively, or even predominantly, by personal interests. No, in the general mass they are magnanimous, responsive, enterprising... In their depths are various unformulated tendencies grounded in heroism and still only awaiting application. It is upon these moods in particular that the newest kind of Soviet patriotism is nurturing itself. It is undoubtedly very deep, sincere and dynamic..." (Chapter 7).

More scurrilous attacks on socialism

All this, however, is only a prelude to a vicious denunciation of the Soviet regime, a negation of Soviet achievements and everything socialist, and a distortion – nay a downright falsification – of Soviet history. Having been forced to pay lip service to socialism having "demonstrated its tight to victory, " to the Soviet state having achieved "ten years successes unexampled in history," Trotsky devotes the rest of his book to a vitriolic attack on the USSR and its leadership. We are told, despite all the admissions about "successes unexampled in history", that "the Soviet State in all its relations is far closer to a backward capitalism than to communism" (p. 22); that, far from achieving the lower stage of communism, what the Soviet Union had achieved was a "**preparatory** regime **transitional** from capitalism to socialism." (p. 52); that this regime was engendering increasing inequalities: "wage differences in the Soviet Union," he asserted, "are not less but greater than in the capitalist countries" (p. 228); and that industry was dominated by a "corps of slave drivers" (p. 229). Before this transitional regime could develop in the direction of socialism, it was absolutely necessary for there to be "a second supplementary revolution against bureaucratic absolutism" (p. 272) because "the bureaucracy can be removed only by a revolutionary force. And, as always there will be fewer victims the more bold and decisive is the attack" (p. 271). Since the Soviet leadership had the overwhelming support of the working class and the collectivised peasantry, Trotsky's references to revolutionary force" could either mean acts of terrorism against the leadership of the Bolshevik Party, or a military conspiracy, or foreign intervention for the overthrow of the Bolshevik regime – or a combination of all these means.

That this is precisely what Trotsky had in mind is made clear in the course of the pages of this book.

Re-assertion of the discredited theory of 'permanent revolution'

There is also the inevitable statement that the advance towards socialism depends to some extent on the prior victory of the revolution in the rest of Europe (p. 274) – a rehash and latest version of Trotsky's permanent hopelessness that masquerades as the theory of 'permanent revolution. That being the case, one may be forgiven for asking- what will the "supplementary revolution against bureaucratic absolutism" achieve if the revolution is destined to vegetate and degenerate into hopelessness in the absence of "victory of the revolution in the rest of Europe"?

In addition, the book contains virulent denunciations of all attempts at raising the productivity of labour, unattainable under the conditions of capitalism Trotsky attacks all wage differentials, piece-work payments, socialist emulation drives – all of which are simply denounced as "a source of injustice, oppression; and compulsions for the majority, privileges and a 'happy life' for the few" (pp. 244-245). Apart from the demagogy of it all, what comes through is the sheer ignorance, not to mention dishonesty: it would appear that its author has failed totally to grasp the essence of *The Critique of the Gotha Programme*, in winch Marx deals, inter alia, with the norms of distribution under the lower and higher stages of communism In the lower stage, distribution can only be according to the formula From each according to his ability, to each according to his work, a formula which does not "remove the defects of distribution and inequality of 'bourgeois right'" (Lenin, *State and Revolution*).

Equating socialism and fascism and spreading defeatist demoralisation

Driven by his intense and insensate hatred of the Soviet state, mindless subjectivism and limitless vindictiveness against the Bolshevik regime for the reason that the latter had decided to expel him for his incorrigible factionalism, Trotsky goes to the despicable length of saying in Chapter 11 of his book *Revolution Betrayed* that "Stalinism and fascism ... are symmetrical phenomena In many of their features they show a deadly similarity."

In the appendix to his book, Trotsky says:

"...with the working class and its sincere champions among the intelligentsia... our work will actually cause doubts and evoke distrust – not of the revolution but of its usurpers. But that is the very goal we have set ourselves."

Trotsky predicts and calls for the defeat of the USSR in war

Since Trotsky, driven by a combination of egotistical factionalism and bourgeois subjectivism, always referred to the Leninist leadership of the Bolshevik party and the Soviet state as a "Stalinist bureaucracy", "caste of usurpers", "totalitarian Regime", etc., it can hardly be denied that the purpose and intention behind Trotsky's demented vituperations was to malign the Soviet regime by attempting to convince workers all over the world that this regime, indistinguishable according to Trotsky from fascism, was not deserving of their support. Such an attitude is only the prelude to wishing, and calling, for the defeat of this regime in any war against fascism by spreading demoralisation. That Trotskyism took this step not only secretly but also openly is clear from the following disgusting pronouncements concerning the then impending Second World War. In these pronouncements Trotsky predicts with malicious glee the military defeat of the USSR in the coming war. Indeed he goes even further, asserting that a protracted war without a military defeat "would have to lead to a bourgeois-Bonapartist revolution." Here are Trotsky's very words:

"Can we, however, expect that the Soviet Union will come out of the coming great war without defeat? To this frankly posed question we will answer as frankly; if the war should only remain a war, the defeat of the Soviet Union will be inevitable. In a technical economic, and military sense, imperialism is incomparably more strong. If it is not paralysed by revolution in the west; imperialism will sweep away the regime which issued from the October Revolution" (*Revolution Betrayed*, p. 216).

What would be the case if the Soviet Union managed to survive the fate assigned to it by Trotsky? Well, the destruction of the Soviet state would ensue just the same. Turn or twist as we may – military defeat or not – the Soviet Union could not survive the war:

"The protracted nature of the war," Trotsky wrote, "will reveal the contradictions of the transition economy of the USSR with its bureaucratic planning.... [I]n the case of a protracted war accompanied by the passivity of the world proletariat the internal social contradictions of the USSR not only might lead but would have to lead to a bourgeois-Bonapartist revolution." (*The Fourth International and the War*).

In 1940, nearing the end of his life – a life full of irreconcilable hostility towards Leninism – Trotsky, with a zeal worthy of a better cause, again predicted the defeat of the USSR and the triumph of Hitlerite Germany:

"We always started from the fact that the international policy of the Kremlin was determined by the new aristocracy's... incapacity to conduct a war.

"...the ruling caste is no longer capable of thinking about tomorrow. Its formula is that of all doomed regimes 'after us the deluge'...

"The war will topple many things and many individuals. Artifice, trickery, frame-ups and treasons will prove of no avail in escaping its severe judgment" (Statement to the British capitalist press on *Stalin – Hitler's Quartermaster*).

"Stalin cannot make a war with discontented workers and peasants and with a decapitated Red Army" (*German-Soviet Alliance*).

"The level of the USSR's productive forces forbids a major war... The involvement of the USSR in a major war before the end of this period would signify in any case a struggle with unequal weapons.

"The subjective factor, not less important than the material has changed in the last years sharply for the worse...

"Stalin cannot wage an offensive war with any hope of victory.

"Should the USSR enter the war with its innumerable victims and privations, the whole fraud of the official regime, its outrages and violence will inevitably provoke a profound reaction on the part of the people, who have already carried out three revolutions in this century...

"The present war can crush the Kremlin bureaucracy long before revolution breaks out in some capitalist country..." (*The Twin Stars: Hitler-Stalin*).

Trotsky's predictions refuted by the epic victory of the USSR in World War II

As usual, and happily for humanity, all Trotsky's predictions were totally belied. After initial reverses in the first few weeks of the war, attributable in the main to the Nazi surprise attack, the Soviet defences stiffened. Before long they struck back. The rest of the world, like Trotsky, had given the USSR only a few weeks before collapsing in the face of the onslaught of the allegedly invincible Nazi war machine. The Red Army and Soviet people, united as one under the leadership of the CPSU and their Supreme Commander Joseph Stalin, exploded this myth of Nazi invincibility. Soviet Victories in the titanic battles of Moscow, Stalingrad, Kursk and Leningrad will forever be cherished not only by the peoples of the former, great and glorious Soviet Union, but also by all progressive humanity.

"The Battle of Moscow had been an epic event... It had involved more than 2 million men; 2,500 tanks, 1,800 aircraft, and 25,000 guns. Casualties had been horrifying in scale. For the Russians it had ended in victory. They had suffered the full impact of the German 'Blitzkrieg' offensive and, notwithstanding their losses... they had been able to mount an effective counter-attack. They had begun to destroy the myth of German invincibility..." (Ian Grey, *Stalin – Man of History*, Abacus, p. 344).

The surrender on 1 February 1943 at Stalingrad, by the fascist general Von Paulus and 23 other generals, mesmerised the world. The victory of the Red Army at Stalingrad was incredible as it was heroic. The Nazi losses in the Volga-Don-Stalingrad area were 1.5 million men, 3,500 tanks, 12,000 guns and 3,000 aircraft. Never before had the Nazi war machine, which was accustomed to running over countries in days and weeks, suffered such a humiliating defeat, a defeat "in which the flower of the German army perished. It was against the background of this battle... that Stalin now rose to almost titanic stature in the eyes of the world" (Deutscher, *Stalin*, p. 472). From now on nothing but defeat stared the Germans in the face, leading all the way to the entry of the Red Army into Berlin and the storming by it of the Reichstag on 30 April 1945 – the same day that the Fuhrer committed suicide. Six days later, Field- Marshall Wilhelm Keitel, acting on behalf of the German High Command, surrendered to Marshall Zhukov.

Stalin and the Great Patriotic War

Although the credit for the victory must correctly be given to the Soviet armed forces and the heroic efforts of the Soviet people, no narrative of these fateful years is complete without a reference, indeed a fulsome tribute, to the undisputed leader of the CPSU(B), the Soviet people, and the Supreme commander of the Soviet forces Joseph Stalin. Even a renegade like Gorbachev is obliged, apropos the Soviet victory in the Second World War, to admit that: "A factor in the achievement of victory was the tremendous political will purposefulness and persistence, ability to organise and discipline people, displayed in the war years by Joseph Stalin." (*Report at the Festive Meeting on the 70th Anniversary of the Great October Revolution* held in Moscow on 2 November 1987, p. 25).

Ian Grey, who is a bourgeois but honest writer, has this to say on this score:

"The massive setbacks and the immediate threat to Moscow would have unnerved most men, but the impact on Stalin was to strengthen his grim determination to fight. No single factor was more important in holding the nation from disintegration at this time." (*Ibid.* p. 335).

Further:

"It was in a real sense his [Stalin's] victory. It could not have been won without his industrialisation campaign and especially the intensive development of industry beyond the Volga. Collectivisation had contributed to the victory by enabling the government to stockpile food and raw materials to prevent paralysis in industry and famine in the towns. But also collectivisation with its machine-tractor stations, had given the peasants their first training in the use of tractors and other machines." (*Ibid.* p. 419).

Quoting Isaac Deutscher, who is far from being friendly to Stalin, approvingly, Ian Grey continues:

"'Collectivised farming had been 'the peasants' preparatory school for mechanised warfare'...

"It was his victory, too, because he had directed and controlled every branch of Russian operations throughout the war The range and burden of his responsibilities were extraordinary, but day by day without a break for the four years of the war he exercised direct command of the Russian forces and control over supplies, war industries, and government policy, including foreign policy." (*Ibid.* pp. 419-420)-

Finally the same writer says:

"It was his victory, above all because it had been won by his genius and labors, heroic in scale The Russian people had looked to him for leadership, and he had not faded them. His speeches of July 3 and November 6, 1941, which had steeled them for the trials of war, and his presence in Moscow during the great battle of the city, had demonstrated his will to victory. He... inspired them and gave than positive direction. He had the capacity of Wending to detail and keeping in mind the broad picture and, while remembering the past and immersed in the present; he was constantly looking ahead to the future"(p. 424).

Innately hostile as he is to Stalin, Deutscher is nevertheless obliged to Paint this Picture of Stalin's role during the war:

"Many allied visitors who called at the Kremlin during the war were astonished to see on how many issues, great and small military, political or diplomatic, Stalin personally took the final decision. He was in effect his own Commander-in-Chief, his own minister of defence, his Own quartermaster, his Own minister of supply, his own foreign minister, and even his own *chef de protocole*. The *stavka*, the Red Army's GHQ, was in his offices in the Kremlin. From his office desk; in constant and direct touch with the commands of the various fronts, he watched and directed the campaigns in the field From his office desk, too, he managed another stupendous operation, the evacuation of 1,360 plants and factories from western Russia and the Ukraine to the Volga, the Urals and Siberia, an evacuation that involved not only machines and installations but millions of workmen and their families Between one function and the other he bargained with, say, Beaverbrook and Harriman over the quantities of aluminium or the calibre of rifles and anti-aircraft guns to be delivered to Russia by the western allies; or he received leaders of the guerrillas – -- from German occupied territory and discussed with them raids to be carried out hundreds of miles behind the enemy's lines At the height of the battle of Moscow, in December 1941, when the thunder of Hitler's guns hovered ominously over the streets of Moscow, he found time enough to start a subtle diplomatic game with the Polish General Sikorski who had come to conclude a Russo-Polish treaty... He entertained them [foreign envoys and visitors] usually late at night and in the small hours of the morning. After a day filled with military reports operational decisions, economic instructions and diplomatic haggling he would at dawn pore over the latest dispatches from the commissariat of Home Affairs, the NKVD... Thus he went on, day after day, throughout four years of hostilities – a prodigy of patience tenacity, and vigilance, almost omnipresent almost omniscient." (Isaac Deutscher, *Stalin*, pp. 456-457).

And further.

" ...[T]here is no doubt that he was their [the Soviet troops] real Commander-in-Chief .His leadership was by no means confined to the taking of abstract strategic decisions, at which civilian politicians may excel The and interest with which he studied the technical aspects of modern warfare, down to the minute details, shows him to have been anything but a dilettante. He viewed the war primarily from the angle of logistics ... To secure reserves of manpower and supplies of weapons, in the right quantities and proportions, to allocate them and transport them to the right points at the right time, to amass a decisive strategic reserve and to have it ready for intervention at decisive moments – these operations made up nine-tenths of his task" (*Ibid.* p. 459).

Deutscher also dispels any notion of popular hostility to the Soviet regime:

"It should not be imagined that a majority of the nation was hostile to the government If that had been the case no patriotic appeals, no prodding or coercion, would have prevented Russia's political collapse, for which Hitler was confidently hoping The great transformation that the county had gone through before the war had... strengthened the moral fibre of the nation. The majority was imbued with a strong sense of its economic and social advance, which it was grimly determined to defend against danger from without." (*Ibid.* p. 473)

So much then for the Trotskyist drivel about the "new aristocracy's incapacity to conduct a war," the "discontented workers and peasants and a decapitated army" making it impossible to make a war, the alleged inferiority of the weapons of the Red Army, Stalin being unable to "wage an offensive war with any hope of victory," and the war crushing "the Kremlin bureaucracy."

Far from being crushed, the Soviet regime emerged from the war much strengthened. Far from crushing the Soviet regime by its war against the USSR, the Nazi regime itself was crushed, as was Germany. What is more, the Soviet victory demonstrated beyond measure the correctness the policies of industrialisation. and collectivisation pursued, in the teeth of Trotskyist and imperialist opposition, by the Soviet regime before the war.

"The new appreciation of Stalin's role did not spring only from afterthoughts born in the flush of victory. The truth was that the war could not have been wan without the intensive industrialisation of Russia; and of her eastern provinces in particular. Nor could it have been won without the collectivisation of large numbers of farms. The muzhik of 1930, who had never handled a tractor or any other machine, would have been of little use in modern war. Collectivised farming with its machine-tractor stations, had been the peasants' preparatory school for mechanised warfare. The rapid raising of the average standard of education had also enabled the Red Army to draw on a considerable reserve of intelligent officers and men. We are fifty or a hundred years behind the advanced countries. We must make good this lag in ten years. Either we do it, or they crush us – so Stalin had spoken exactly ten years before Hitler set out to conquer Russia. His words, when they were recalled now, could not but impress people as a prophesy brilliantly fulfilled as a most timely call to action. And, indeed a few years' delay in the modernisation of Russia might have made all the difference between victory and defeat. " (Deutscher, *Ibid.* p. 535).

This is how Deutscher captures the victory parade in Red Square at the end of the war.

"On 24 June 1945 Stalin stood at the top of the Lenin Mausoleum and reviewed a great victory parade of the Red Army which marked the fourth anniversary of Hitler's attack. By Stalin's side stood Marshall Zhukov, his deputy the victor of Moscow, Stalingrad, and Berlin. The troops that marched past him were led by Marshall Rokossovsky. As they marched rode, and galloped across the Red Square regiments of infantry cavalry, and tanks swept the mud of its pavement – it was a day of torrential rain – with innumerable banners and standards of Hitler's army At the Mausoleum they threw the banners at Stalin's feet .The allegorical scene was strangely imaginative...

"The next day Stalin received the tribute of Moscow for the defence of the city in 1941. The day after he was acclaimed as 'Hero of the Soviet Union' and given the title of Generalissimo." (*Ibid.* p. 534)

In "these days of undreamt-of triumph and glory," continues Deutscher: "Stalin stood at the full blaze of popular recognition and gratitude. These feelings were spontaneous, genuine not engineered by official propagandists slogans about the 'achievements of the Stalinist era' now conveyed fresh meaning not only to young people, but to sceptics and malcontents of the older generation..." (*Ibid.* p. 534).

Thus, at the end of the war Trotskyism stood thoroughly discredited - thoroughly bankrupt – and regarded as no more than an information bureau and anti-communist ally of imperialism in particular during the US-led war of aggression against the Korean people, during which most Trotskyists, consumed by their genetical hatred of the Soviet Union, effectively sided with US imperialism and against the forces of national liberation and socialism.

The cold war – Imperialism's response to the prestige of victorious socialism

The USSR's successes in the collectivisation of agriculture, massive socialist industrialisation, gigantic achievements in education, science, technology and culture, with a continuously rising standard of living for the working class and the collective peasantry, and her crowning victory in the anti-fascist Great Patriotic War, with the resultant victory of Peoples Democratic governments in Poland, Hungary Czechoslovakia, Romania, Bulgaria and Albania, brought Soviet prestige to soaring point. It was this spectacle of triumphant, confident and advancing socialism that put the fear of God into the hearts of the imperialist bourgeoisie and caused the latter, under the leadership of US imperialism which had emerged from the war as the strongest imperialist power, to initiate the cold war, establish the NATO aggressive warmongering military alliance and re-arm West Germany as a member of this alliance.

The NATO warmongers threatened the USSR with an economic blockade and nuclear blackmail. But the USSR defied the blockade and military threats alike. It re-doubled its efforts to build its economy and destroy the US monopoly of the atom bomb. At the end of September 1949, in the same week as Comrade Mao Tse-tung proclaimed the Peoples Republic of China and the success of the Chinese revolution, the world heard the detonation of the USSR's first atom bomb. Even such a Trotskyite writer as Isaac Deutscher, whose hatred for Stalin is total and who never misses a chance of describing Stalin as "dug and dreary", is obliged to admit:

"He [Stalin] achieved some of his vital objectives. He resisted Western pressures firmly enough to deter any American design for spreading the war, and Soviet nuclear industry progressed by leaps and bounds and produced its first hydrogen bomb in 1953, shortly after the Americans had achieved the feat. The basic sectors of the Soviet economy, having reached their pre-war level of output in 1948-49, rose 50 per cent above in Stalin's last years. The modernisation and urbanization of the Soviet Union was accelerated. In the early fifties alone its urban population grew by about 25 millions Secondary schools and universities were giving instruction to twice as many pupils as before 1940. Out of the wreckage of the world war the foundations had been re-laid for Russia's renewed industrial and military ascendancy, which was presently to startle the world" (*Stalin*, pp. 585-586).

A few pages further down, Deutscher observes:

"... it is a fact that 'Stalin found Russia with a wooden plough and left her equipped with atomic piles'... This summary of Stalin's rule is, of course, a tribute to his achievement." (*Ibid.* p. 609). The words quoted by Deutscher are quoted from his own obituary of Stalin published in the Manchester Guardian of 6 March 1953.

Of course, only the demented Trotskyites can argue that the above achievements took place automatically on the foundation of socialist property relations inherited from the October Revolution – not because of but despite, the leadership, as it were. No, such achievements do not come without correct leadership. One has only to compare the leadership, the policies pursued by the leadership, and the consequences and achievements of those policies, in the USSR up to the mid-fifties with those of the leadership from the 20th Party Congress (1956) onwards until the August 1991 coup resulting in the disintegration of the USSR to realise what a chasm divides the two periods. Even Roy Medvedev, no friend of Stalin's and the author of the thoroughly anti-Stalin *Let history judge*, has been obliged to say- "Stalin found the Soviet Union in ruin and left it a superpower. Gorbachev inherited a superpower and left it in ruin."

Triumph of Khrushchevite revisionism and the resuscitation of Trotskyism

Thus, in view of her gigantic achievements, winch were the fruit of domed persistence in following the Leninist path of socialist construction, working people treated with utter contempt the Trotskyist ravings against the USSR and its leadership. All this, however, changed with the triumph of Khrushchevite revisionism in the CPSU after the death of Stalin. Khrushchevite revisionism could get nowhere in its desire to undermine socialism, reach an accommodation with imperialism, and start the long process, on the road back to capitalism, unless it attacked the person who had, after the death of Lenin and in a bitter struggle for the victory of the Leninist line on the question of socialist industrialisation and collectivisation, become the most representative spokesman of, and whose name was indelibly and inextricably linked with, the building of socialism in the USSR, namely, Joseph Stalin. Hence Khrushchev's attack on Stalin in his so-called secret report to the 20th Party Congress of the CPSU in 1956. With this attack on Stalin's alleged 'personality cult' – all, incidentally, in the name of Leninism and with the alleged purpose of returning to true Leninist norms – began the long political and economic process that brought forth ripe capitalist fruit under the loving and tender care of Khrushchev's last successor, Gorbachev I cannot here go further into this question, with which I have dealt in greater detail in my *Perestroika – the Complete Collapse of Revisionism*.

Khrushchev's attack on Stalin brought some retrospective credence to Trotskyist counter-revolutionary fulminations against the USSR from the mid-twenties onwards. As under the tutelage of Khrushchev and his successors, the CPSU itself, as well as the revisionist parties in Europe and elsewhere, really did begin to degenerate, the long-repeated Trotskyist jeremiads about the alleged Thermidor and degeneration gripping the CPSU from 1923 onwards came to acquire the semblance of plausibility.

Trotskyism sides with every single counter-revolutionary movement

In the aftermath of the triumph of revisionism at the, 20th Party Congress of the CPSU, and under its direct stimulus, bourgeois-nationalist tendencies within the working-class parties, acting in close coordination with the imperialist agencies and broadcasting media as well as the church, came to the fore in some of the Peoples Democracies. In a number of places – most notably Hungary – these led to counter-revolutionary uprisings. Everywhere in these upheavals directed against socialism and the rule of the working class, the Trotskyites were, as was to be expected, on the side of imperialism reaction, counter-revolution and clerico-fascism. The XIth World Congress of Trotskyites paid homage to the CIA-Vatican inspired and led Hungarian counter-revolution in the following glowing terms:

"The Hungarian revolution of October-November 1956 went the farthest on the path of a fully-fledged anti-bureaucratic political revolution." (*Imprecor*, Nov. 1979).

James Burnham, the American Trotskyist, and Trotsky's trusted henchman until 1940, openly advocated, from 1950 onwards, the US policy of 'liberation" of captive nations" – a policy of destabilising People's Democracies in eastern Europe.

Trotskyism and the Czechoslovak counter-revolution

When the extreme revisionists in Czechoslovakia, under the leadership of Dubcek, impatient with the slow speed of 'reform' aimed at restoring a capitalist economy and a multi-party bourgeois democracy, started the, so-called Prague Spring they euphemistically declared that their aim was "to free Marxism from Stalinist and bureaucratic distortions" and to "formulate the humanist vocation of the communist movement." The meaning of these apparently attractive slogans became all too clear during 1989, by which time the liquidation of the Communist Parties in Poland and Hungary, the dismantling of what remained of socialist planning of the economy in those countries, and the plunge into capitalism and bourgeois democracy, under the tender mercies of imperialism and its spiritual arm, the Vatican, had become obvious. Dubcek, in a letter to the Party leadership, pleaded with them not to condemn reforms in Poland and Hungary. So did his colleague, Jiri Pelikan, who called upon the "democratic movement in western Europe [to] develop a dialogue with Solidarnosc... in Poland, with the Democratic Forum ... in Hungary, with Charter 77... in Czechoslovakia", that is, with the forces of capitalist restoration. Then, in 1968, as well as subsequently in the late 1980s and the beginning of the present decade, the Trotskyites, true to form, were to be found on the side of counter-revolution.

The Trotskyist, Petr Uhl, was one of the most active members of the anti-communist Charter 77. On 15 October 1988, the luminaries of Charter 77 and other opposition groups signed a Manifesto of the Movement for Civil Liberty which, *inter alia*, demanded "economic and political pluralism," – freeing of business from "the yoke of centralised bureaucracy," "complete reestablishment of private enterprise in... commerce craft industry, small and medium business," and "the integration of the Czech economy... in a natural way with the world economy, based upon the international division of labour" – that is, a manifesto for the restoration of capitalism and bourgeois democracy. While declaring himself to be in sympathy with this manifesto of the velvet counter- revolution, Uhl did not judge it opportune. to append his signature to it, even criticising it as "liberal democratic" and "totalitarian." The conclusion? Instead of denouncing it and disassociating himself from it, he welcomed the manifesto because of the inclusion in it of "the demand for worker's control in the big firms," of the kind that abounds in the imperialist countries with its humbug of a share-owning democracy.

After the success of the counter-revolution and the implementation of the above manifesto, Uhl stated:

"One might discuss the extent to which Trotsky's theory of the political revolution has been justified. I think that it is in Czechoslovakia that the reality is nearest to this theory."

He goes on to add by way of an explanation of this 'political revolution' and the composition of this anti-communist coalition: "so long as people can say they are against communism, Stalinism and bureaucracy, then everybody is in agreement" (*Imprecor*, no. 304, 1990, p. 26).

And further: "There were those who saw in Charter 77 a step in the direction of political revolution – of whom I was one; others saw in it a means of propagating the word of Christ. It was a veritable laboratory of tolerance." (*Imprecor,* no. 300, 1990, p. 8).

Comrade Ludo Martens, Chairman of the Belgian Party of Labour (PTB), in his book *The Velvet Counter Revolution* which I recommend to any reader desiring a detailed account of these events, justly remarks in this regard

"To overthrow and destroy socialism (whether it be a strong and vigorous socialism or an eroded and sickly socialism), the clerico-fascists reactionary nationalists, the agents of the CIA and social democrats all stick together and needless to say they show great 'tolerance' towards those pseudo-socialists who back up their political agitation with repeated quotations from Trotsky" about the so-called anti-bureaucratic, political revolution, which turns out, as it was always meant, to be no more than another expression, wrapped up in 'left' verbiage, for the simple restoration of capitalism Thus has Trotskyism arrived at its "political revolution" against "Stalinist bureaucracy"!!

The Belgian Trotskyist, Ernest Mandel, greeted the events of 12 January 1990 as: "the sudden access of hundreds of millions of men and women from the Eastern countries to political life." (*Imprecor*, no. 300, 1990, p. 8). The meaning of this meaningless hyperbole was made clear by the selfsame puffed-up and pompous Trotskyist gentry a mere ten months later, on 23 November 1990: "According to Petr Uhl there are probably only a few thousand, even a few hundred militants from Civic Forum at the regional and local level."

Further: "The student movement which largely inspired the events of November 1989, no longer exists." (*Imprecor*, no. 319, 1990, p. 4).

In Czechoslovakia, the "access to political life", over which Mandel waxes so lyrical, happened at a time when the masses were following the counter-revolutionary Civic Forum, under the leadership of Havel, a notorious CIA agent. This is what Pavel Pechacek, head of the Czech section of the CIA-financed Radio Free Europe, has to say in this instance:

"We have always played important role. According to the leader the student revolt in Bratislava, it was Radio Free Europe which lit the fuse. We always had close contacts with Havel, Camogursky and Dienstbeir, who today are members of the new government but who for years worked for us as independent correspondents."

These were the people – the Havels and Pechaceks – who "awakened the masses to political life" in Czechoslovakia. Knowing full well that the Civic Forum stood for restoration of capitalism, that Vaclav, Klaus, head of the Civic Forum Since October 1990 and one of the principal advisors to Havel, is not Only on record expressing his admiration for Milton Friedman and Hayek the two bourgeois economists most admired by Ronald Reagan and Margaret Thatcher, former President Of the USA and former Prime Minister of Britain respectively, but also his commitment to "a market economy, without qualification" – knowing all this Mandel told a Belgian financial paper on 21 March 1990:

"The transition to a completely western model is possible, but this is not the case in countries like the Soviet Union and Czechoslovakia" (*De Financieel Ekonomische Tijd*, 21.3.90).

Knowing all this, why did the Trotskyists go along with the Civic Forum? Their innate hatred of socialism and communism is the answer. This truth is blurted out by the dim-witted Uhl, who explained that his support for the Civic Forum and Havel was motivated by a desire to get rid of the remnants of the socialist system!

After several political somersaults and mental contortions, the Trotskyist Uhl finally, and not unexpectedly, carved for himself a nice little niche in the 'new bourgeois Czech state, as the head of the Czech Press Agency, a position to which he was appointed in February 1990, from which to propagate the wonders of capitalist restoration and the "access to political life" set in train by this restoration – 'anti-bureaucratic revolution' if you like.

From jabbering away about worker's control only the previous day, Uhl had little difficulty in getting on with the job of informing the masses that the Czech state represents society:

"It a generally understood that, if we depend on the State, we support the government which is not exactly the case. Of course we must 'respect' the government but if there is a conflict it would be up to a parliamentary committee to make a decision, because parliament represents the State more than the government does Our task is to propagate news abroad about Czech society This is the concern of the Czech State because it represents Czech society for the moment." (*Imprecor*, no. 304, 1990, p. 27).

If this drivel amounts to anything at all it amounts to the worst form of parliamentary cretinism, according to winch the, Czech parliament and bourgeois Czech state are synonymous, and since, according to this Trotskyist imbecile, the state represents society, it is "our task to propagate news abroad about Czech society."!! This is the beginning and end, the sole meaning of the much-trumpeted Trotskyist "anti-bureaucratic, political revolution." Nothing could be clearer than this.

The Belgian Trotskyist Mandel and the French Trotskyist Broué crudely defend counter-revolution

Mandel, notorious for his anti-Marxism and vulgar economism, had for more than two decades held the view that in the absence of a violent counter-revolution capitalism could not be restored in the socialist countries. Proceeding from this erroneous premise, he has all along advocated multi-party democracy (democracy for all). Since, according to his reasoning, there was no danger to socialism and the real enemy lay in 'bureaucracy', through multi-party democracy socialism would acquire a democratic character. Towards the end of 1989, in regard to the counter-revolutionary movement in Timisoara, which resulted in the overthrow and foul murder of Ceaucescu and his wife, Helena, Mandel surpassed even the lying imperialist media in denouncing the "hideous Stalinist crimes in Timisoara" – crimes which turned out not to have been committed after all. The bourgeois media's inflammatory figures of 70,000 to 100,000 dead in Timisoara, and the horror stones about mass graves, turned out to be totally fabricated. The correction, of only 700 deaths, most at the hands of the army rather than the Securitate, was made in half-inch columns relegated to inside pages.

In regard to the counter-revolutionary movement in the German Democratic Republic Mandel declared.

"I am delighted over what's happening in Berlin. The anti- socialist movement is really weak." Welcoming this "revolution," – he went on to exclaim. "Everything Trotsky ever hoped for could now become reality." (*Dans Humo*, 21.12.89).

In Trotskyist, as indeed in imperialist circles, whereas Gorbachev, Yeltsin and Trotsky are revolutionaries, Stalin and the Bolshevik party that he led are counter-revolutionaries!!

It is worth while reproducing the views of Mandel, considered to be the theoretician of the Trotskyist IVth International, on the counter-revolutionary Programme of capitalist restoration embodied in Gorbachev's Perestroika. During an interview he gave to a journalist of *New Times* he was asked:

"Is it not true that Mikhail Gorbachev stated that Perestroika is a true new revolution?"

To which Mandel replied: "Yes, he does indeed and again this is very positive. Our movement has defended this thesis for 55 years and was therefore labelled as counterrevolutionary. Today people, both in the Soviet Union and in a large part of the international communist movement, understand better where the real counterrevolutionaries were." (no. 38, 1990, French edition).

Again, in the same Belgian financial paper already referred to, Mandel expresses himself on this question in the following terms:

'The reformer Yeltsin represents the tendency which wants to reduce the gigantic state apparatus. Consequently he follows in Trotsky's footsteps." (21 March 1990).

These wonderful admissions from the Trotskyist Mandel, for which we thank him heartily, only make our job of exposing Trotsky's anti-communism and anti-Bolshevism, easier. For once, Mandel is absolutely correct. Gorbachev, Yeltsin and Trotsky do have the same ideological and political physiognomy – they all stand for capitalist restoration.

This same despicable Mandel had earlier described the arch reactionary monarchist, Sakharov, as one of the "radical and progressive left" and the bourgeois-nationalist Sajudis of Lithuania as belonging to "the radical democratic and nationalist popular movement"!! (*Imprecor*, no. 285, 3 April 1989).

Without exception, all the Trotskyists everywhere supported the counter-revolutionary brainchild of the CIA and the Vatican, Solidarnosc in Poland, cheering its rise and accession to power – again in the name of Trotsky's "anti-bureaucratic political revolution,"

The French Trotskyist Broué, already referred to, for his part applauds the counter-revolutionary movements of eastern Europe which two years after the publication of his Trotsky came to head the capitalist-restorationist regimes, and correctly attributes to Trotsky the following version of "political revolution."

"The demands appearing in these movements of workers and youth reconstitute those that defined the program of political revolution' as Trotsky sketched it: democracy, freedom for parties, destruction of the bureaucratic apparatus, 'free 'trade unions, electoral freedom and the right of criticism ending infringements on human tights, punishing those responsible for crimes, winning the democratic rights of speech, assembly, demonstration, as well as the appearance of a free – and hence stimulating -press." (*op. cit.* p. 943).

The American Trotskyist ICL's sophisticated defence of counter-revolution

Of course the correct and candid representation by Messrs Mandel and Broué of Trotsky's 'political revolution" against "Stalinist bureaucracy" is highly embarrassing to the Spartacists of the ICL, who are forever presenting a sanitised version of Trotskyism in an effort to gain for the latter some credibility in the eyes of progressive workers in order to be able to carry out all the more successfully the propagation of counter-revolutionary Trotskyism and the theory of permanent hopelessness. That is why they fly into a rage against Mandel and Broué's straightforward admissions of the simple truth.

What is the ICL's own position? While it may appear to an unwary or superficial observer that they defend the gains of socialism and socialist construction, and workers' states, this is not the case. They are second to none in maligning the former socialist regimes, especially the Soviet regime from 1923 to 1953, which they have always denounced as "bureaucratic", needing to be overthrown by a "political revolution." In unguarded moments, however, dropping their usual mask, they reveal the reactionary essence of their Trotskyist political line. In an article written in November 1992 for the sole purpose of presenting a sanitised version of Trotskyism, the truth literally oozes out, despite themselves, in the following lines:

"The idea that 'socialism' could be built in a single country (and a backward one at that), surrounded by imperialist enemies, is a nationalist perversion of Marxism.

"Stalin's dogma of 'socialism in one country' was the ideological afterbirth of a political counterrevolution which **defeated** Leninist internationalism and brought to power a nationalist bureaucratic caste."

Was the idea of socialism in a single country really a "nationalist perversion of Marxism " was it really "Stalin's dogma" and "the ideological afterbirth of a political counterrevolution which **defeated** Leninist internationalism and brought to power a nationalist bureaucratic caste"? If what Spartacist says is true, would it be worthwhile for them, or for anyone else, to defend the gains of this "nationalist perversion"? The Spartacists of the ICL only had to ask this question to realise that they were giving away their whole game, of appearing to defend socialism in words while undermining it in deeds. Are the Spartacists really so ignorant of Lenin's writings as not to realise that this "nationalist Perversion" of socialism in one country was not

"Stalin's dogma," but Lenin's? He and he alone must get the credit (or discredit) for the authorship of this 'dogma'. The Spartacists ought not to be so ignorant, for they claim that they are Leninists and make the same claim for their guru, Trotsky. Let them then read Lenin's 1916 article *Military Programme of Proletarian Revolution*, and his article on cooperation at the beginning of 1923, just as Trotsky was writing his anti-Leninist, counter-revolutionary pamphlet New Course. And let them read the following lines taken from Lenin's 20th November 1922 speech to the Moscow Soviet:

"We have approached the very core of the everyday problems, and that is a tremendous achievement. Socialism is no longer a matter of the distant future, or an abstract picture, or an icon. Our opinion of icons is the same – a very bad one. **We have brought socialism into everyday life** and must here see how matters stand. That is the task of our day, the task of our epoch. Permit me to conclude by expressing confidence that difficult as this task may be, new as it may be compared with our previous task and numerous as the difficulties may be that it entails, we shall all – not in a day, BUT IN A FEW YEARS – all of us together fulfil it whatever the cost **so that NEP Russia will become socialist Russia**." (V.I. Lenin, *Collected Works*, Vol. 33, p. 443 – Emphasis added).

After this, if the Spartacists have the courage of their convictions, they ought to accuse Lenin of the "dogma" they attempt to pin on Stalin's shirt sleeve; they ought to lay the blame for this "nationalist perversion" at the doorstep of Lenin rather than depositing it at Stalin's.

SWP Trots welcome the demise of communism

The largest British Trotskyist Organisation, the Socialist Workers Party (SWP), having cheered every counter-revolutionary movement in eastern Europe from the CIA-Vatican inspired Hungarian uprising to the capitalist restorationist Solidarnosc and the Civic Forum in Czechoslovakia, greeted with frenzied glee the demise of socialism in the USSR. Its organ, *Socialist Worker*, declared joyfully- "Communism has collapsed. Now fight for real socialism." (31 August 1991). It went on to cheer the toppling of the statues of Sverdlov, Dzerzhinsky, and other "former Communist Party icons"; it even considered it opportune to carry a picture of the statue of the great Lenin down and to declare "Communism has collapsed... It is a fact that should have every socialist rejoicing."

The SWP went as far as to argue that Yeltsin's victory had brought "the workers of the USSR closer to the spirit of the socialist revolution of 1917, not further from it."

Well, since the Berlin wall came down on 9 November 1989, what has this 'death of communism' and the fight for 'real socialism' brought in its trail? Exactly what imperialism had been desiring and working for over decades. Exactly what every intelligent observer, not consumed by anti-communist hate, expected it to be. The market forces have been let loose over the unhappy peoples of eastern Europe and the former USSR. Everywhere there is rising unemployment, contraction of production, catastrophic rates of inflation, national strife, rising racism, anti-semitism and fascism, increased crime, drug trafficking, prostitution, black market and hunger. There has been an astronomic rise in the prices of basic necessities such as food, accommodation, electricity and clothing. In other words, all the freedoms have been unleashed that are associated with a free market economy and the Trotskyite "political revolution" against "Stalinist bureaucracy."

In the former German Democratic Republic, for instance, between the beginning of 1990 and the end of 1991, the economy contracted by 20% as entire industries were shut down. In the first half of 1990, industrial output fell by a huge 40%; in the second half of the same year by another 40%! By the spring of 1991, a third of East Germans had either lost their jobs or were put on short time. From 270,000 in July 1990, unemployment jumped to 1 million by the end of 1991 and 1.5 million in 1992.

In Poland, 2 million workers, representing 15% of the workforce, are un-employed, and, while real wages have fallen by 30% the cost oil living has risen by 40%.

The picture is the same in Hungary and Czechoslovakia, where industrial Production has fallen by a fifth.

In the USSR, which had a giant economy before 1985, industrial production is down by 40% since then; the rate of inflation stands at a staggering 2,500%; the currency is in ruin, with the rouble, which used to have a value higher than the US dollar, now having a rate of exchange of 800 roubles to the dollar (March 1993).

The same goons of the SWP who with such lurid delight greeted the "death" of "communism" as the beginning of the fight for "real socialism" two years later on bemoan, in the manner of innocent virgins, the fact that the changes are hurting the workers. Writing in the *Socialist Worker* of 9 November 1991, they say:

"Wealth, freedom democracy – This, the media claimed, was the future for east Germany as the Berlin Wall came down on 9 November 1989.

"In the weeks which followed Czechoslovaks, Bulgarians and Romanians threw off their Stalinist rulers too. Poles and Hungarians increased the pressure for reform

"Two years on and those same politicians, commentators and pundits are silent. Not one of their predictions has come true, none shows any prospect of coming true.

"...the market economy has not led to prosperity, simply deepened the misery."

On the contrary. Every prediction of bourgeois politicians and media has come true. Capitalism is being restored, and this process, as was known to everyone (including the dim-witted Trotskyists whose "anti-bureaucratic political revolution" against "Stalinism" and "the command economy", shorn of all its 'left' verbiage, amounted to this capitalist restoration), can only take place amid misery and ruin for the masses of workers and an extraordinary enrichment of the few. The movement involving the demolition of all central planning and the introduction of private property cannot but express itself in shocks, jolts and dislocation which are hurting the working class of the former socialist states.

It is indeed the SWP gurus who, if they had any sense of shame and a gram of socialism in them, ought to be quiet at the very least, since it is their darlings, Lech Walesa and his Solidarnosc in Poland, Havel and his Civic Forum in the Czech Republic, Boris Yeltsin in Russia, etc., all leaders of the Trotskyist "anti-bureaucratic revolution", who are introducing the wonders of 'democracy' and the free market'. Instead of wisely keeping quiet, Socialist Worker, having summarised the results of introduction of the market economy in eastern European countries, goes on mildly to complain:

"Yet this, and the misery being suffered in east Germany and Poland, has not stopped Russia's President Boris Yeltsin proposing a programme of rapid and widespread privatisation and the quick removal of food and rent subsidies."

But it would appear that they are not happy with the results as yet, for they believe that the newly established bourgeois regimes have not been thorough enough in destroying all the traces, instruments and institutions connected with the previous regimes in the former socialist states:

"And not a week goes by without revelations proving the hated Stasi, the Securitate, the Hungarian AVO and all the other riff raff which once enforced the Stalinist regimes, are still around"!

The above sentence, apart from revealing that their hatred is most reserved for the socialist regimes, is also a clever attempt to fool the simple Simons, who swell the rank and file of Trotskyist organisations everywhere and who have a weakness for catchphrases, into believing that the former regimes in eastern Europe were Stalinist, i.e., Leninist. In the preface of my book *Perestroika, The Complete Collapse of Revisionism,* referring in this context to the Trotskyites, revisionists and social democrats, I said:

"This revolting gentry – in particular the counter- revolutionary Trotskyites – have been gloating with delirium over the alleged collapse, in Eastern Europe and the USSR, of Stalinism. Just the contrary. What has collapsed is revisionism, and its inevitable degeneration into ordinary capitalism. What is called 'Stalinism' by these despicable creatures is only Leninism in practice. When Leninism was practised in the USSR, as it undoubtedly was during the three decades of Stalin's leadership of the CPSU, it achieved world- historic feats on all fronts – economic, social cultural, diplomatic and military – which is precisely the reason why the very name of Stalin has become the target of so much abuse on the part of the bourgeoisie and its 'hired prize-fighters'. So what has collapsed is revisionism even though in order to confuse the proletariat the sly and yet unthinking and uncouth Trotskyites using the word 'Stalinism' as a swear word rather than as a political characterisation, have been applying it to the very revisionists who entertain mortal haired of Stalin." (pp. viii-ix).

In the end when all is said and done, *Socialist Worker* is well satisfied with the achievements of the counter-revolution in eastern Europe, and ends with the following smug, not to say smutty, conclusion:

"What *Socialist Worker* said in November 1989 remains true today: 'what really wonderful about the new movements in eastern Europe is they raise the possibility of a society which is better, freer and more democratic than that which east or west at the moment'."

In other words, what a wonderful thing it was to have replaced the former socialist regimes with bourgeois regimes and free market economies, the consequences of which Mr Alan Gibson, the writer of this article in *Socialist Worker*, so dementedly and in such self-annihilatory a manner, bemoans!!

The same SWP, which in August 1991 had with great counter-revolutionary zeal declared that Yeltsin's victory had brought "the workers of the USSR closer to the spirit of the socialist revolution of 1917", now declares, through the column of the despicable John Molyneux, that "it is precisely the viciously anti-working class nature of Yeltsin's free market reform, that makes him aspire to dictatorial powers in order to impose his Programme. Consequently no socialist should now support Yeltsin." (*Socialist Worker*, 10 April 1993, "*Russia: should we take sides?*")

Such is the logic of the counter-revolutionary gentry of the SWP: support for Yeltsin's counter-revolution in August 1991 on the pretext that his victory brought the USSR proletariat "closer to the spirit of the socialist revolution of 1917" and opposition to Yeltsin in April 1993 for his attempt to put into effect the declared programme of the very counter-revolution over which the SWP waxed so eloquent!!

Nothing could reveal better the hideous social-democratic face of the SWP than the fact that the same Socialist Worker, which felt elated at the death of communism, suffered a deep "depression" and "post-election demoralisation" in the wake of the fourth consecutive electoral rout of the Labour Party. Bleated the *Socialist Worker:* "The election result was a disaster for everyone who wants a better society."

The crudity of SWP's defence of capitalism and its representatives compelled even the Spartacists of the ICL, another counter-revolutionary Trotskyite organisation, to make the following correct observation:

"An organisation [i.e. the SWP – HB] which found a cause 'that should have every socialist rejoicing' in the victory of Yeltsin's counter-revolutionary forces that have brought poverty, mass unemployment and misery to the masses of the former Soviet Union, while finding a cause to make socialists' sob in the defeat of Neil Kinnock's scab-herding Labour traitors, obviously has a pretty twisted weathervane..." (*Workers Hammer* July/August 1993).

And further down in the same article, continued the ICL: "Capitalist counter-revolution in Eastern Europe and the Soviet Union has meant untold misery for the working masses of those countries – poverty, homelessness and starvation – and made an onslaught of bloody nationalist fratricide. Europe – East and West – faces massive unemployment, the ominous rise of anti-Semitism, racist and fascist terror, attacks on women's fights... Now that the unifying thread of anti-Sovietism no longer mutes their rivalries the imperialist ruling classes are trying to tighten the screws of exploitation on the proletariat at 'home'. At the same time, they try to sell the lie to the working class and oppressed that 'communism is dead' that any attempt to overthrow this system of exploitation and oppression is condemned in advance, useless, even criminal.

"The SWP presents itself as a fighting alternative. If there were any justice in this world, these Third Camp renegades should feel ashamed to even try to show their face in public! From Poland to East Germany to Moscow, they were among the foremost cheerleaders for the forces of counter-revolution that are now devastating Eastern Europe and the ex-Soviet Union. While most of the rest of the left followed suit howling along with the imperialist wolves in championing any and every anti-Soviet 'movement' the SWP not only supported some of the darkest forces of reaction but offered them as a model for the struggle against Stalinist 'totalitarianism.'

"So, for example, following the Soviet withdrawal from Afghanistan the Cliffites heralded the CIA-funded Islamic reactionaries who are now drowning any shred of social progress in that country in blood. *Socialist Worker* (4 February 1989) enthused that a 'Mojahedin victory will encourage the opponents of Russian rule everywhere in the USSR and Eastern Europe'! By rights the SWP should now be pleased that just such 'opponents of Russian rule', i.e., vicious nationalist reactionaries, fascist terrorists, women-hating clericalists, have been unleashed by capitalist counterrevolution." (*ibid.*)

The SWP may be organised independently, but in terms of its programme and political and ideological physiognomy it is indistinguishable from the social-democratic Labour Party – as indeed are all Trotskyite organisations, which everywhere act as an anti-communist militant wing of social democracy.

The hypocrisy of SWP's fake anti-Labour stance is exposed by another Trotskyite, Sean Matgamna. Writing in the *Socialist Organiser* of 19 November 1992, from a perspective which would have the SWP within the Labour Party to help build the 'left' within it, this is how he tears the mask of false anti-Labourism, from the hideous face of the SWP:

"In the 1979 General Election the SWP while proclaiming itself 'the socialist alternative' to the Labour Party declined to put up candidates, backed the Labour Party!... It fell to Foot in a much-quoted interview in the London Evening Standard, to express the SWP's dualism, the approach which left the political labour movement to the right wing in all its crassness. He said: 'For the next three weeks I am a strong Labour supporter. I am very anxious that a Tory government shouldn't be returned, and I shall be going around to meetings we are having telling everyone to vote Labour' (*9 April 1979*)."

Concludes Mr Matgamna: "In his role of SWP ambassador to the bourgeoisie and the media Foot often blurts out the truth about the SWP's politics without the usual 'socialist' obfuscation and phrase-mongering, Michael Foot's nephew Paul is thus a useful man to have around."

The Healyite Trotskyites detect Trotsky's line and welcome Gorbachev's *Perestroika*

The late and unlamented child molester and recipient of funds from a wide variety of sources ranging from the Arab regimes to the CIA for his lifelong devotion to the cause of anti-communism and anti-Sovietism, namely the Trotskyite Gerry Healy of the old and notorious Socialist Labour League (SLL), welcomed Gorbachev's perestroika and glasnost as "the political revolution for restoring Bolshevik world revolutionary perspectives." Since the collapse of the Soviet Union and its disintegration, Healy's followers, the Redgrave Trots of the so-called Marxist Party, have gone on to blacken all Soviet development and history by asserting that Lenin had been wrong throughout and that Rosa Luxemburg's denunciation of Lenin as a "sterile overseer" aiming at "blind subordination" to "an intellectual elite hungry for power" through "pitiless centralism" was correct.

With the disappearance of the former socialist states and the coming to power of bourgeois regimes, the Trotskyites are at sixes and sevens as to how to explain away their wretched theory of "anti-bureaucratic political revolution." As a result they are at each other's throats. The other offshoots of Healy's lunatic fringe, the Northites and Torrancites, are in convulsions over this. The Northites simply pass the buck on to Trotsky who, they say, got it wrong for there was nothing left with which to have a revolution:

What was destroyed between 1936 and 1940 was not only the flower of Marxism but its roots.

"It doesn't detract anything from Trotsky's work to say that he simply could not have known, even when he was writing his denunciations of the Moscow Trials, the scale of the bloodbath that was taking place in the USSR."

This can mean one of two things: either that socialism had ceased to exist and capitalism had been restored by the end of the 1930s, in which case, the Northites appear to be arguing Trotsky ought to have then denounced the Soviet regime far more vehemently than he actually did; alternatively it could mean that the workers' state, albeit a 'distorted! one, continued to exist in the USSR but that after the Moscow treason trials there was no 'revolutionary vanguard' left capable of effecting the Trotskyist 'political revolution', and that therefore the 'overthrow of the bureaucracy' could only lead to the establishment of capitalism, to which end the Trotskyists, with their theory of 'political revolution' have worked all these years. In this case, Trotsky was also wrong in advocating his 'political revolution' thereby leading his followers up the blind alley which leads to capitalist restoration. Whichever way one looks at the above Northite quotation, one comes to the conclusion that these gentry are as much at sea in explaining the momentous developments in the USSR as they are at home with Trotskyist gobbledygook.

From the anti-Soviet defeatism, hidden by veritable phrase-mongering and a pretended belief in the chimerical "anti-bureaucratic political revolution", the Northite Trots pass over without any difficulty to the following unreserved and absolute defeatism, characterising the whole period from October 1917 onwards as one of unmitigated disaster:

"We should avoid using phrases that become hackneyed from over-use; but in this case it can truly be said that we have come to the end of an entire historical period that was opened in 1917".

Their rivals, from the Torrance faction of Trots, the *Newsline* Workers' Revolutionary Party (WRP) rump, do not like the Northite 'explanation' whose utter defeatism greatly embarrasses them. In an attempt to gain some credibility for Trotskyism and overcome doubts even among the Trotskyist rank and file as to whether their guru Trotsky's theory of "political revolution" and his lifetime spent in anti-Soviet activity ever contained an iota of progressive, let alone revolutionary, content, the Torrancites come down, Mandel fashion, in favour of characterising the counter-revolutionary developments in the former USSR and eastern Europe as "revolutionary" in nature. Deriding the Northites, the Torrancites write:

"The comic side of all this is that since the bureaucracy is the 'determining force', if the so-called 'military industrial complex' were to overthrow Yeltsin, reinstating the USSR, then no doubt North would have to declare that the USSR was once again a workers state. He would have to say 'Thank god for the Stalinist bureaucracy.'"

Thus we find one section of Trots (the Northites) blaming Trotsky for not being firm enough in his fulminations against the Soviet Union, thereby misleading his followers into the blind alley of supporting an allegedly workers' state in need of political revolution, when, say the Northites, socialism had already been destroyed and therefore there was nothing left against which to have a revolution. The other section (Torrancites) exonerate themselves from all responsibility for lifelong anti-Soviet and anti-communist activity by pretending that the counter revolution has not taken place at all, that Yeltsin represents the "political revolution", which, in the course of time, will "restore Bolshevism."

Some other Trots

For its part, the Trotskyist rag Socialist Organiser, referred to immediately above, exulted over the victory of the Yeltsin forces thus: "His brave defiance of the Stalinist establishment will help workers to see what the issues are – an opening society, with the beginnings of the rule of law and some degree of democratic self-control, on one side, and stifling ice-age Stalinist dictatorship on the other." (*SO Supplement*, 20 August 1992).

The 'Militant' Trotskyites were no less despicably shameless in welcoming the Yeltsin counter-revolution: "All over the world workers will see this as people's power reducing the threat of dictatorship to a poorly scripted farce. Every dictator will tremble at the prospect of his own subjects taking such action."

'Workers Power', yet another Trotskyist outfit, being fully cognisant of the "socially counter-revolutionary nature of Yeltsin's programme" and the "spivs and racketeers" who supported him, nevertheless felt obliged to back Yeltsin: "No matter what the socially counter- revolutionary nature of Yeltsin's programme, no matter how many spivs and racketeers joined the barricades to defend the Russian parliament, it would be revolutionary suicide to back the coup-mongers and support the crushing of democratic rights...

"It is far better that the fledgling workers' organisations of the USSR learn to swim against the stream of bureaucratic restorationism than be huddled in the 'breathing space' of the prison cell."

Looking forward with great enthusiasm "to the next stage – the task of rapidly dismantling the instruments of central planning" (*Workers Power*, September 1991), 'Workers' Power', reducing its counter-revolutionary logic to an absurdity, calls for "workers control of the counter-revolution! – for a "workers Yeltsin" who will not stop half way:

"Revolutionaries share the workers' hatred for all the real and symbolic representatives of their oppression. We support the closing down of the palatial CPSU offices, private shops and sanatoria, the rooting out of the KGB officers. But we put no trust in Yeltsin or the leadership of the main soviets in the chief towns and cities to carry out the destruction of the Stalinist dictatorship.

"We seek at every point to involve the masses independently in the process of the destruction of the CPSU dictatorship...

"The workers must control the process of destruction of the Stalinists through to the end and not let Yeltsin preserve what is useful to him."

Like the *Socialist Organiser*, it – Workers Power – too was fully aware of the forces supporting Yeltsin. Its on the spot report stated that those manning the Yeltsin barricades "were not for the most part, the most audacious workers and students of Moscow," adding:

"Rather they were in the majority small businessmen, speculators and owners of ['free enterprise'] co-operatives, the traditional base of the [Russian nationalist] 'Democratic Russia' demonstrations, plus a few hundred young enthusiasts. While there have been reports of strike action and mass mobilisations in other parts of the USSR, in Moscow at least the working class played little part in the resistance to the coup".

There are, of course innumerable other Trotskyist groups of which nothing, at all has here been said. It is not, however, either possible or necessary or even desirable to make reference to all of them, for they represent no more than variations on themes already encountered in the brief sketch given above of the major Trotskyist tendencies. What unites them all, however, is that they are all Trotskyists. They are, therefore, all counterrevolutionary to their finger tips – not out of a desire to be so, but because they cannot help being counter-revolutionaries for as long as they follow Trotsky's petty bourgeois, pessimistic and counter revolutionary theory of 'permanent revolution.'

The bankruptcy of Trotskyism and the triumph of socialism

The events of the last few years, which have overwhelmed eastern Europe and the USSR, have not only proved the utter bankruptcy of Khrushchevite revisionism but also exposed, if such exposure was ever required, the thoroughly counter-revolutionary nature of Trotskyism. These events have proved beyond doubt the inner affinity, notwithstanding the differences in form, of revisionism and Trotskyism. Khrushchevite revisionism, right in form and in essence, was aiming, through the Communist Party, for the same aim of restoring capitalism in the USSR and other east European countries that Trotskyism, 'left' in form and right in essence, had been attempting ever since the twenties through the so-called "anti-bureaucratic revolution." This affinity, and the proof in practice in a most vivid form of the counter-revolutionary essence of revisionism and Trotskyism, ought to facilitate the task of exposing and fighting both these counter-revolutionary trends.

We are, however, passing through a time of ideological decay, confusion, disintegration and wavering – a time when renegacy and apostasy are the order of the day. With the complete collapse of Khrushchevite revisionism, the disintegration of the USSR and the east European socialist regimes, as well as the liquidation of the revisionist parties elsewhere, the Trotskyists can yet again be expected to come forward and say: 'We told you so. Trotsky was correct in asserting that socialism could not be built in a single country, etc.' Our task is to refute this nonsensical and counter-revolutionary chatter. The collapse of the USSR, far from proving the correctness of Trotskyism, actually smashes it to smithereens. What it proves is that had Trotskyism (or Bukharinism for that matter) been put into effect in the USSR in the mid-twenties, the latter would have collapsed much earlier, more than six decades ago. The CPSU, however, rejecting Trotskyism and Bukharinism, went on to construct socialism and a mighty Soviet state – a bastion and a beacon of socialism whose epic achievements in war and peace, whose heroic feats in all spheres of social development, economic, educational, artistic, military and scientific; whose superhuman endeavours to build a new society based not on the exploitation of one human being by another but on the basis of the law of balanced development of the national economy for the satisfaction of the constantly-rising needs of the population, a society based on fraternal cooperation and not on national strife and racism, a society based on sex equality not on sex discrimination; whose titanic struggle against, and crowning victories over, Hitlerite Germany – victories which freed humanity from the scourge of fascism – brought socialism to eastern Europe and imparted a tremendous impulse to the national liberation movements thereby weakening imperialism; and whose unstinting support to the revolutionary proletarian and national-liberation wars else -where, whose proletarian internationalism, will continue to inspire humanity in its endeavour to get rid of all exploitation and achieve a classless communist society through the dictatorship of the proletariat.

Trotskyism or Leninism?

In this period of ideological confusion, the Trotskyites are bound to come forward with scraps of pompous, high-sounding, empty, obscure and bombastic catchphrases which confuse the intelligentsia and non-class-conscious workers, in an attempt to fill the ideological vacuum and to pass off Trotskyism as Leninism. They are bound to make yet another attempt to substitute Trotskyism for Leninism. They must not be allowed to do this. Every Marxist-Leninist, every class-conscious worker, must play his or her part in frustrating this attempt and in ensuring that it fails as miserably as did all similar attempts in the past.

It is by way of a contribution to frustrating this attempt to substitute Trotskyism for Leninism that this book is presented. The author seeks no other reward than the fulfilment of this aim. The choice is straightforward: either counter-revolutionary Trotskyism or revolutionary Leninism. One or the other. Trotskyism or Leninism?

A few words about this book

Finally, a few words as to the material which constitutes this book. Parts

I to IV are based on a series of lectures which I delivered in London at the invitation of the Association of Communist Workers (ACW), an anti-revisionist group which, although small in numbers, played a very important role in defending the fundamentals of Marxism-Leninism against attacks from Trotskyists and revisionists alike. Originally these pages were distributed as a series of four separate pamphlets under the title *Some Questions Concerning the Struggle of Counter- Revolutionary Trotskyism Against Revolutionary Leninism.* The pages dealing with the Spanish Civil War (Part V) were never produced at the time. Since then, on the basis of some of the notes that I had at my disposal and further research on her part, my comrade and friend Ella Rule wrote this section and presented it as a paper to the deliberations of the Stalin Society on 24th March, 1991. The sections dealing with the question of collectivisation and class struggle under the conditions of the dictatorship of the proletariat were both written by way of a preface to collections of Stalin's writings on these two important questions. These too appeared as separate pamphlets, the one on collectivisation in 1975 and that on class struggle in 1973. In this last pamphlet, the section dealing with the German-Soviet Non-Aggression Pact has been much expanded to include substantiating evidence which was not in the original pamphlet. Now that this Pact has come in for renewed criticism, I have decided to include this material. Also, I have updated the text to take account of works which have been published since the original material was produced, or have come to my notice since that time. From the context, and the dates of the publications referred to, the reader will have little difficulty in spotting the new material.

These last two publications were necessitated by a stream of attacks on the Marxist-Leninist policies of the CPSU(B) during the leadership of Stalin (1924-53) from individuals and organisations who called themselves anti-revisionist and, therefore, by definition- ought to have been opposed to revisionism as well as Trotskyism. What these people were putting forth in practice, however, was something incredibly confused and incredibly reactionary – in many cases merely a rehash of Trotsky's propositions. Their writings were characterised by a mixture of erroneous platitudinousness and ignorant arrogance. The British anti-revisionist movement of those days really did go in for a considerable amount of "sublime nonsense", to borrow Engels' expression, producing several personages who gave themselves airs about the science of Marxism-Leninism of which they really never learnt a word.

In the 1870s, in the preface to his *Anti-Dühring*, Engels complained bitterly about the "infantile disease" which was then afflicting a large section of the German intelligentsia, including a section of the socialist intelligentsia, where "Freedom of science is taken to mean that people write on every subject which they have not studied and put this forward as the only strictly scientific method."

This "infantile disease" was rampant among a large section of the 1970s anti-revisionist movement and its fellow travellers, causing great confusion. Again, at the invitation of the ACW, I edited the two collections of Stalin's writings on the subjects referred to above, provided each collection with a lengthy preface with the purpose of refuting the sublime nonsense and platitudes of our opponents who, possessing but little knowledge of the science of Marxism-Leninism but a goodly amount of conceit and ignorance, were dishing out, in the name of Marxism, a great deal of muddled and reactionary nonsense. Since this reactionary nonsense came from quarters at least nominally anti-revisionist, it had to be dealt with.

A long time has passed since the contents of this book were first published in the form of six separate pamphlets. Some of the persons polemicised against have either died or retired, or have simply, and wisely, retreated into the little bourgeois niches they have carved for themselves. Equally, some of the organisations have either gone into voluntary liquidation or faded into political oblivion. Yet others are no longer recognisable as they have changed their names once or more often (this being especially true of the Trotskyite organisations). None of this matters in the least. What is really important are the issues and questions which were then, and show every sign of becoming now or in the future, the subject of heated arguments and polemics. In that case all we need to do is to remove the name of the person or organisation while using the substance of the argument against those who might insist on putting out nonsense of the type which was put forward by the people I polemicised against two decades ago. Moreover those against whom I polemicised are insignificant today, or were perhaps insignificant even at that time. But similar nonsense has come from quarters far more significant, whose word carries weight, influence and authority. It is my hope that my polemics against my opponents will have the desired effect of countering equally pernicious nonsense from these high quarters.

Originally, when the contents of this book were distributed as separate pamphlets, each pamphlet was provided with an introduction, so that each could be read on its own if so desired. That form is maintained in the book now presented. This ought to make it easier for the reader to read different sections of the book in any preferred order. I have deliberately provided a rather lengthy preface in order, first, to bring the text up to date by including a brief reference to the demise of socialism in the USSR and eastern Europe, as a culmination of a long process of revisionist theory and practice in the fields of politics, political economy, class struggle and philosophy, all set in train by the triumph of Khrushchevite modem revisionism at the 20th Party Congress of the CPSU in 1956; second, to provide more evidence of the thoroughly counter-revolutionary nature of Trotskyism by reference to the response of present-day leading Trotskyite organisations and individuals to the restoration of capitalism in eastern Europe; and finally to provide to all the matters dealt with in this book a degree of coherence which, being originally issued as separate pamphlets, they perhaps did not possess.

It has been decided, also, to provide three appendices – one on what has come to be called Lenin's Testament, another on the relations between Trotsky and the imperialist press and another on the murder of Trotsky by one of his own followers. As they are self-explanatory, there is no need to say anything about them here.

With these words I conclude this preface by expressing the hope that it will make for a useful contribution, no matter how small, in the struggle against Trotskyism and revisionism, and in defence of the eternally true propositions of Marxism-Leninism. I make no pretensions to any originality whatsoever in writing this book. What I have to say in it will be common knowledge to the older generation of Marxist-Leninists. But, to our shame, knowledge of what ought to be generally-known truths is becoming less and less with the younger generation. We meet young comrades who want to join the movement and help with our work. What are we going to do with these comrades? I answer this question in the following words of Stalin's: "I think that systematic reiteration and patient explanation of the so-called 'generally known' truths is one of the best methods of educating these comrades in Marxism." (Stalin, *Economic Problems of Socialism in the USSR*, FLPH Peking, p. 9).

If I have succeeded in correctly and systematically reiterating at least some of the so-called 'generally-known' truths in this book, I shall consider myself entirely satisfied with the enterprise involved.

Notes

1: **Otzovists**: an opportunist group formed in the RSDLP in 1908. It was led by A. Bogdanov. From behind a screen of revolutionary verbiage, the Otzovists demanded the recall of the Social-Democratic deputies from the Third Duma (Czarist parliament) and the cessation of Party activity in legal and semi-legal organisations, maintaining that because reaction was on the rampage the Party had to confine itself to illegal work.

This would have isolated the Party from the masses and turned it into a sectarian organisation incapable of mustering the forces for another revolutionary upsurge.

Lenin showed that the views of the Otzovists were inconsistent, unprincipled and hostile to Marxism. At a conference of an extended editorial board of the Bolshevik newspaper, *Proletary*, in June 1909, a resolution was passed to the effect that "as a clear-cut trend in the RSDLP Bolshevism has nothing in common with Otzovism or ultimatumism" (a variety of Otzovism). A. Bogdanov, the Otzovist leader, was expelled from the Bolshevik Party.

2: **Liquidators**: representatives of an opportunist trend in the RSDLP during the period of reaction from 1907-1912. The Mensheviks were utterly demoralised by the defeat of the revolution of 1905-7. They wanted the disbandment of illegal Party organisations and the cessation of underground revolutionary activity. Their aim was to liquidate the revolutionary Party of the working class and set up an openly reformist party. The liquidators urged the working class to come to terms with the bourgeoisie, to reconcile itself to the reactionary regime in Russia.

The liquidators were headed by Martov, Axelrod, Dan, Martynov and other Menshevik leaders. Trotsky in fact sided with the liquidators.

At the Sixth (Prague) All-Russia Conference of the RSDLP (January 1912), the liquidators were expelled from the Party.

3: **AUCCTU**: The All-Union Central Council of Trade Unions.

4: "Among these legends most be included also the very widespread story that Trotsky was the 'sole' or 'chief organiser' of the victories on the fronts of the civil war. I must declare, comrades, in the interest of truth, that this version Is quite out of accord with the facts. I am far from denying that Trotsky played an important role in the civil war. But I must emphatically declare that the high honour of being the organiser of our victories belongs not to individuals, but to the great collective body of advanced workers in our country, the Russian Communist Party. Perhaps it will not be out of place to quote a few examples. You know that Kolchak and Denikin were regarded as the principal enemies of the Soviet Republic. You know that our country breathed freely only after these enemies were defeated. Well, history shows that both these enemies, i.e., Kolchak and Denikin, were routed by our troops IN SPITE of Trotsky's plans.

"Judge for yourselves:

"**Kolchak**: This is in the summer of 1919. Our troops are advancing against Kolchak and are operating near Ufa. A meeting of the Central Committee Is held. Trotsky proposes that the advance be halted along the line of the River Belaya (near Ufa), leaving the Urals In the hands of Kolchak, and that part of the troops be withdrawn from the Eastern Front and transferred to the Southern Front. A heated debate takes place. The Central Committee disagrees with Trotsky, being of the opinion that the Urals, with its factories and railway network, must not be left In the hands of Kolchak, for the latter could easily recuperate there, organise a strong force and reach the Volga again, Kolchak must first be driven beyond the Ural range Into the Siberian steppes, and only after that has been done should forces be transferred to the South. The Central Committee rejects Trotsky's plan. Trotsky hands in his resignation. The Central Committee refuses to accept it. Commander-in-Chief Vatsetis, who supported Trotsky's plan, resigns. His place is taken by a new Commander-in-Chief, Kamenev. From that moment Trotsky ceases to take a direct part in the affairs of the Eastern Front.

"**Denikin**: This Is In the autumn of 1919. The offensive against Denikin is not proceeding successfully. The 'steel ring' around Mamontov (Mamontov's raid) is obviously collapsing. Denikin captures Kursk. Denikin is approaching Orel. Trotsky is summoned from the Southern Front to attend a meeting of the Central Committee. The Central Committee regards the situation as alarming and decides to send new military leaders to the Southern Front and to withdraw Trotsky. The new military leaders demand 'no Intervention' by Trotsky in the affairs of the Southern Front. Operations on the Southern Front, right up to the capture of Rostov-on-Don and Odessa by our troops, proceed without Trotsky.

"Let anybody try to refute these facts."

(Stalin, *Collected Works*, Vol. 6, pp. 350-352)

www.ingramcontent.com/pod-product-compliance
Lightning Source LLC
Chambersburg PA
CBHW062159290526
45791CB00017B/1228

* 9 7 8 1 3 8 7 9 6 9 3 3 3 *